In the Maker's Hands

POWER HOUSE

In the Maker's Hands

How to Turn Devastation to Breakthrough and Shape Your Best Life!

Joyce B. Respers

Cover art by Sarah Fernandez for POWER HOUSE. ©2023 Power House Studios, LLC. (See Appendix for cover inspiration tribute.)

Published by: **Power House**

An imprint of Power House Studios LLC.

thepowerhousestudio.com

PO Box 101678 Cape Coral FL 33910

Home of *The Power House Blueprint*™ Concierge Publishing System

Endorsements

Apostle Dr. Respers has written one of the most challenging books I've ever read. She skillfully and methodically takes the reader through the various stages of Christian growth that are so vital to our preparation for the Master's use in His Kingdom. She shares her personal experiences and struggles with moderate transparency to encourage the reader to stay in the process.

Although the various stages carry a measure of pain, shaping, and breaking, the benefits of enduring hardness as good soldiers far outweighs any pain, frustrations, and failures from our past. The Lord is calling the Body of Christ to mature, develop, and grow up in our stance against the enemy of our souls.

As Christians, we know that someway, somehow, all things will work together for our good. We also know that if we suffer with Him, we shall also reign with Him. So gird up the loins of your mind and get ready for God to **turn your devastation into a breakthrough as He shapes us for our best life.** Stay *In the Maker's Hands!*

– Apostle Dr. Albert Evans, Jr.
Presiding Prelate, International Fellowship of Covenant Churches and Ministries

This book is a must have! The author gives an insightful and in-depth understanding of God's Word, His purpose, and His plans for us before we were born! You will begin to recognize the Lord's appointed times for great healings and deliverances in your life! I love the way the author describes her personal experiences with Holy Spirit as He lovingly helped her through each process and stage of her growth. There was no condemnation or contempt from our Heavenly Father, only patience and love. This book is relevant for all ages—kids, beginners, or babes in Christ, those who are questioning their identity and purpose, leaders, teachers, mothers, fathers, and even grandparents—this book contains truths essential to every believer's personal relationship with Jesus Christ.

– **Kimberly King, Minister/Teacher**
Family Outreach Word of Deliverance Ministries Inc.

In the Maker's Hands is a prophetic word of release to the Body of Christ! Now is the set time to abide, grow, and stay *in the Maker's hands.*

I remember when Apostle Joyce would share a few nuggets from her book with me, and I would say, "I need to read your book *now!*" Well, Glory to God *now* is here. God raised Apostle Joyce up to be His voice of destiny for this generation and beyond because she knows she was chosen from the gutter-most for His utmost! We thank you, Lord Christ because we have all had those "just in time" moments in our life (like

Apostle Joyce shared in her book), and remember we are all *chosen on purpose* and *set apart to His good pleasure.*

As readers journey through this book, we pray that we each would allow the season of refreshing to fall on us as we continue to have *daily visits to the Potter's house.*

What a fantastic labor of love and strength, Apostle Joyce. We love and honor you for this gift!

– Prophetess Dr. Audrey M. Brown

In the Maker's Hands was such a beautiful reminder that God is in control, and has nothing but great things planned for me! He is painting the story of my life one stroke at a time. As in viewing unfinished art, it may appear not to make sense or have any depth to it, but once the painting is done, EVERYTHING flows as it should and illuminates life in a form that does not REQUIRE words! I have truly been encouraged by the powerful words, scriptures, and affirmations in this book! Thank you Dr. Respers for explaining the importance of knowing 'who and whose' you are in the simplest form. With love and respect,

– Prophetess Dr. Latasha Kornegay
Bible Faith Global, Inc.

Readers will immediately gravitate to the pages of this book as Dr. Respers eloquently, through the Holy Spirit, invites the audience to find healing from the oppositions in their lives and freedom from whatever is stopping them from walking out their God given purpose and destiny. Whether you are a leader in the church or a layman, her transparency along with her step-by-step approach will lead you to ask, "Do I know who I am?" And also to discover the answer as to who we are as God reveals our true identity.

The analogy that she uses (that we are the clay *in the Maker's hands,* broken and marred) brings encouragement and empowerment to better understand God's process. She further points out that every child of God must be discipled by mature spiritual leaders and how they are not to rush the process at the expense of the result. Here and only here we will find that we are His Masterpiece.

– Apostle Dr. Dee Dee Swindell

God has invited us, His spiritual creation, to partner with him in revealing to mankind His great love and plan of salvation, transformation and empowerment for all! God has put the essence of Himself, His creative and transforming power into the hearts of all those who will believe. Now is the time to step up and walk in the spiritual authority that we already have, in ways like never before!

We all have been made in His likeness/image and every believer has been gifted with all that is needed to fulfill their God ordained purpose in the earth. Accordingly, when we begin to operate in the fullness of the Spirit of Life in Christ Jesus, lives are transformed, the Great Commission is fulfilled, and God gets the glory! However, sadly, there are many believers who remain unsure of themselves, hesitant, or even paralyzed by fear. As a result, they have not stepped up and begun to walk in the right and power that Christ died to give us; too many still are not enjoying the triumphant, abundant life that is God's plan for every Spirit filled believer. But this book provides a way forward.

In her book, *In the Maker's Hands,* Dr. Joyce Respers methodically and effectively writes about how to receive and manifest the fullness of life in Christ Jesus. She emphasizes that sanctification (becoming Christ-like) is a process of yielding and submitting to the Potter like vessels of clay *in the Maker's hands.* Dr. Respers covers several key aspects of God's transforming process—a divine process that is not bound by what you've done or by where you've been! I highly recommend this empowering book. It is a must-read that requires an open mind and the fervent prayer, *"Shape me and mold me! Lord, have your way!"*

– Apostle Dr. Sean A Swindell

This book is certainly a must-read for every believer. It is not unusual to see such professional academic works in the secular arena. It is, however, very unusual to see such an element of professional academics in the Christian world. God uses Dr. Respers to take us on a spiritually educated odyssey into the making of true believers. She expounds on the intimacies and definitive structure of every believer's essence.

In the Maker's Hands has a very strong apostolic impartation. Dr. Joyce imparts a spiritual foundation with an emphasis on spiritual character and integrity. She uses not only sound structure but also sound doctrine, employing the appropriate scriptures to identify and confirm all that we (as believers) should walk in. This book stirs us to become all our Lord Jesus Christ wants us to be. It is definitely a road map required for the fullness of every believer's journey of faith.

We look forward to many other works of faith to follow. Again, there are not enough words to express the definitive spiritual accuracy and integrity of this book. It defines the true meaning of God as the master builder of all of his children. Dr. Joyce Respers, job well done, "thou good and faithful servant." Certainly, an even greater reward is awaiting you in your future.

– Apostle Dr. Alfred Kornegay
Bible Faith Global, Inc.

Dedication

I dedicate this book to the memory of my mentor, the late Reverend Hubert Morris. He was an anointed, loving teacher employed in my early ministry development. He taught me how to study and rightly divide the Word of God while studying for my Theology Degree. Father God allowed him to deposit His divine impartation in my life. These deposits later caused me to launch out into the deep to go forth in the ministry.

As I started to go forth, Reverend Morris was my friend, counselor, and source of strength. He believed in me when I struggled with my insecurities. He encouraged me to go after God's vision for my life. His wisdom was beyond the years of many other instructors. I am grateful to have had such a unique mentor, teacher, and spiritual father who directed me when I did not know what to do. His investment in my life was instrumental in forming and shaping me, impacting my present life-path and even my destiny (my future destinations). His gift of love and patience will forever be remembered in the Kingdom of our dear Lord. For that, I appreciate him even more. I pray this book honors his memory, and I look forward to a reunion in Christ in the ages to come.

Acknowledgments

I want to acknowledge Jesus Christ, my Lord and Savior, in all I do and am today.

I want to acknowledge my mother, Mattie J. Blount, my rock in a hard place. Through the years, it has been your strength and tenacity that have been my major influence.

I thank God for my husband, Billy Respers, who is my love. Thank you for allowing the Holy Spirit to direct you while assisting me in every endeavor I aimed to accomplish in the Kingdom of God. You never stood in God's way while He led me to complete His will for my life; rather, you trust in God and believe in the anointing on my life. Thank you so much. You helped motivate me and gave me the desire to keep going and remain focused during this journey.

I want to acknowledge my spiritual fathers, who also equipped me for the work of the ministry:

Reverend Hubert Morris (deceased), in whose memory I dedicate this first book;

Dr. Willie Grant (deceased) was present as a leader during my foundational seasons; he taught me how to trust God through tough times and challenging situations. The process was not always simple and easy; nevertheless, it was what I needed from my spiritual father;

And finally, Apostle Dr. Alfred and Dr. Latasha Kornegay. I thank you both. I was embarking on twenty-odd years of ministry when God brought you into my life. I had temporarily lost focus on God's assignment for my life. I had almost completely given up on the ministry. You were (and still are) instrumental in my life when I needed someone to believe and trust in the anointing of Jesus to further me in my assignment. You pushed me out of my comfort zone. And perhaps most importantly, you placed a demand on the anointing of Jesus *in me* on a higher level—a level that I did not even realize was available in my life.

Preface

The time is at hand for *a bold mental breakthrough*. I realized it afresh, even while writing this book.

God will give us strategies for whatever is needed to transform us into His image. We need God's confidence, wisdom, and divine strategies to assist us with our family, finances, children, jobs, health, marriages, and other relationships. Fear is a tool of our greatest enemy, intended to erode (steal, kill, or destroy) our confidence, wisdom, and strategies. But we can have courage! We need not fear the enemy attacking us, even the enemy named *terror*. Paul, the apostle, stated that you can live "without being frightened in any way by those who oppose you. This is a sign to them that they will be destroyed, but that you will be saved—and that by God" (Philippians 1:28 NIV). In other words, we can and must stare fear in the face and say, "Not here!"

We must take a definitive attitude when the enemy comes to attack us. Why do we allow intimidation to control us? Often it is because we suffer from poor self-esteem—we do not know who we are. We cannot afford to be wimps (weak and timid) in this season of our lives.

In Jeremiah 33:3 (AMPC), the Lord says, "Call to Me and I will answer you and show you great and mighty things, fenced in and hidden, which you do not know (do not distinguish and recognize, have knowledge of and understand)."

We must call unto the Lord; He said He would never let you be in a situation where He will not be with you. We must be willing to ask God to help us in His plans for our lives in every situation. The Word of the Lord is always our compass and gives us a visual picture of this help and protection:

> The Lord is my Shepherd [to feed, guide, and shield me]; I shall not lack. He makes me lie down in [fresh, tender] green pastures; He leads me beside the still and restful waters. He refreshes and restores my life (my self); He leads me in the paths of righteousness [uprightness and right standing with Him— not for my earning it, but] for His name's sake. Yes, though I walk through the [deep, sunless] valley of the shadow of death, I will fear or dread no evil, for You are with me; Your rod [to protect] and Your staff [to guide], they comfort me. (Psalm 23:1–4 AMPC)

We all will go through struggles, but we do not have to fear because the Lord—our Master Potter—is with us. He is our source, identity, and present help in trouble.

In Jeremiah 29:11 (AMPC), the Lord declares, "For I know the thoughts and plans that I have for you, says the

Lord, thoughts, and plans for welfare and peace and not for evil, to give you hope in your final outcome."

Plans come to us from angelic visitation, by receiving the Word of God speaking to us, or through prophetic declaration. However, we must allow God's Word to renew our minds (change our thoughts) so that we choose to agree with His will. The Kingdom's stratagems (carefully worked out plans of action) are recognizing and obeying God when He gives us directions. But to obey, we must know the direction is from the Lord. Sometimes it may not make sense; however, we must be in tune with the Holy Spirit.

As we discover in the pages ahead, He is our Potter, we are the clay, and we cannot afford to doubt the voice of God. God will give us favor with people who will go out of their way to help us because we obey Him. We must obey immediately because postponement and procrastination are equivalent to disobedience.

Once we hear His voice, we must decide how we will respond. We cannot respond like the story of the rich young ruler in Mark 10:17–27, unwilling to leave his life of wealth for the greater wealth of following Jesus. We cannot respond despondently; we must respond quickly. We must not respond like the blind man at the pool of Siloam in John 9:1-11, using excuses and waiting for someone else to take action on our behalf, or as he was, waiting on others to put us in the water or waiting for the angel to stir the waters. We must not depend on others to do what He has called us to complete, nor can we rely on people to provide what only our Heavenly Father can.

We must trust, depend on, and obey the Lord... our Potter. While turmoil and uncertainty rock the global cultures, it is time for believers in Jesus Christ to lay aside all anxieties, refuse to be intimidated, and not let offenses stop us. I am certain that is why the Lord impressed upon me to release this book at this specific season. As I pen the pages of this book, my prayers are, "Lord, allow your voice to inspire me, move me with quick obedience, and let the words in this book help someone."

I share my heart now by His Grace and with urgency.

Contents

Introduction

I have always been curious about the handiwork of our Creator. I admire creation and the beauty of nature. Trying to figure out who God is (and who I am in His creation) has often been a mystery to me. Many of us have lifelong struggles with understanding the Kingdom of God and knowing who we are in His Kingdom. Perhaps it will help you, as it did me, to see yourself as an empty shell to be poured into.

As we take that receiving posture, the Word of God says in 2 Peter 1:3 (AMPC; emphasis added):

> For His divine power has bestowed upon us all things that [are requisite and suited] to life and godliness, through the [full, personal] knowledge of Him Who called us by *and* to His own glory and excellence (virtue).

Further, I believe God will give us *methods* for receiving everything we need. As our Creator, He is always mindful of us. My Lord takes care of my imperfections, struggles, insecurities, and lack of whatever is missing—and I am confident He will provide for you also.

God is calling for the Body of Christ to mature in her destiny. Since God is our Creator, we must not allow anything to cause us to abort our destiny. Satan and his imps will confront our identity and self-worth and try to devalue us. Knowing that my life is always *in the Maker's hands* allows me to stay in perfect peace and security in His presence.

> Without being frightened in any way by those who oppose you, we have no worries. This is a sign to them that they will be destroyed, but that you will be saved—and that by God. Don't be terrified by anything your enemy may bring to you. (Philippians 1:28 NIV)

All types of opposition will come from without and within; however, the greatest often comes from within our carnal or unrenewed minds, wills, and emotions. As we allow Him, God will establish His confidence within us; therefore, as a child of God, we *must believe* that all things are possible.

As you read this book, I pray that you will gain a greater understanding of the perfect will of the Holy Spirit. I encourage you to be pliable in His hands, allowing the Master Potter to chisel, prepare, shape, smooth, and refine you into His masterpiece.

Allow Holy Spirit to guide you through these pages. As you read, allow Holy Spirit to create a hunger and thirst in your heart so that you come out of the experience even more enthusiastic about living your life *in the Maker's hands.*

Our Creator, the King of Glory, wants us to understand how deeply we are loved and who we are in His Kingdom. And, He desires that we begin to function and operate *in the fullness of our assignment*. We also must choose to trust, surrender, and give ourselves *for the benefit of others*. There are hidden gifts in you and me that must be explored and manifested.

Let the truth in these pages (from the Word and the Spirit of God) **turn your devastation into a breakthrough, and let God shape your best life!** I cannot wait to see the finished work, the new vessel—I know it will be most excellent because you are... ***In the Maker's Hands!***

Chapter 1

Who Am I?

If I didn't know the ending of a story, I wouldn't begin. I always write my last lines, my last paragraph, first, and then I go back and work towards it. I know where I'm going. I know what my goal is. And how I get there is God's grace. –Katherine Anne Porter (1890–1980)

Then God said, "Let us make man in our image, after our likeness. And let them have dominion over the fish of the sea and over the birds of the heavens and over the livestock and over all the earth and over every creeping thing that creeps on the earth." (Genesis 1:26 ESV)

Jesus answered them, "Is it not written in your Law, 'I said, you are gods'? If he called them gods to whom the word of God came—

and Scripture cannot be broken—do you say of him whom the Father consecrated and sent into the world, 'You are blaspheming,' because I said, 'I am the Son of God'?" (John 10:34–36 ESV)

Where do I begin? I was born and raised in Maribel, North Carolina. I'm the daughter of Clarence W. Blount (deceased) and Mattie Jones. As far as I can remember, I have always felt I could never fit in with anyone. It was an abnormal feeling. I am one of three children; my brother David Lee Blount and I are fraternal twins. We had an older brother, Clarence W. Blount Jr., who died of an erupted appendix at eight years old. He was very smart and helpful around the house, helping Mom with the chores and doing whatever he could to please her. When I think of him now, I think that he was God's little gift given to us only briefly to bring us peace.

After his death, I assumed the responsibilities of my older brother. I was expected to clean, pick up, wash the dishes, and whatever responsibilities were at hand. I was the one that had to do them. Early in my life, as the eldest cousin in the family, at just ten years old, I was also assigned to babysit all the younger children "down the road" (or so they called it). I am talking about keeping three to four kids and a baby all day. I ordered and bossed the children around and told them when, what, and how to do whatever. My great-grandmother even had to get on me because she said I was too bossy with the younger children. Yet I was expected to perform as an adult and had been forced to carry adult responsibilities. For example, if the children got in trouble, I was held account-able for their wrong actions. Taking on this kind of respon-sibility caused me to act like I was grown before I really was, forfeiting my own childhood.

As I grew, I had a problem with stuttering. I often com-pared myself to others and developed very low self-esteem. This dramatically worsened after I was abused by one of my family members, leaving me feeling worthless and unworthy. Because of both fear and shame, I felt I could never discuss or share this with my mom or anyone. Little did I know that suppressing this incident was the root cause of my insecu-rities, inferiority, and poor self-esteem. Through the years, I could cover up, mask, and function as if everything were normal. I guess that is what I had been taught or had seen that religious people did, and I came from a deeply religious family. When I say religious, I mean no fruits of righteous-ness—just religious works.

We were members of a Baptist church organization. My mom enrolled me in the Baptist Training Union (BTU) program. This was a program for middle-school and high-school-age youth. Youngsters were selected from each church in the Baptist Church Union to represent their church in the community. I was the one chosen from our church. My task was to attend the meetings and then return to the church to share the information. I would share what I had learned with the congregation during the Sunday school class with the age group of my department. I remember that I loved attending the classes and enjoyed studying God's Word. It was not like anything I was accustomed to. Throughout this experience, Jesus had his hand on me, but I did not yet understand that.

I was an honor student in every grade and became Miss Pamlico County during my first year of High School. I enjoyed my high school years, even though my parents' marriage was troubled or, as we called it back then, on the rocks. Eventually, my parents separated after I graduated from high school, and my brother enlisted in the army. Despite the changes, I did not allow that to stop me from succeeding in my studies.

All this mayhem did, however, motivate me to leave home. I decided to enroll in college. I did not particularly care which college; I just knew I was ready to leave home and be independent. Still, the years of turmoil in the family dynamics had left me feeling insecure and intimidated by other people. I had a major problem trying to fit in with others, but surprisingly, I was accepted by my peers at college. I found myself making foolish choices and becoming promiscuous in my behavior. I was so ashamed of these preferences, some of which even led me to dangerous situations. So, even though I went to college to get an education, I was making idiotic choices that were too embarrassing to speak about openly.

Looking back on those days, now later in life and wiser in my ways, I thank Jesus daily for protecting and keeping me safe during those foolish days! Especially in my foolishness, Jesus' love was there to shield me. The Word of God, even the little I knew of it then, was my source of strength.

> The Lord will keep you from all evil; he will
> keep your life. The Lord will keep you going
> out, and you are coming in from this time
> forth and forevermore. (Psalm 121:7–8 ESV)

I can clearly see now that the grace of Jesus kept me safe and alive in those tough times. My first two years of college were wearisome. My mother and father finally went through a divorce. As I mentioned, my brother left home and enlisted in the army, and I continued to fail in many areas of my life. The experiences left me with more insecurities and deficiencies. I had no desire to push myself for excellence.

The third year of college was much better than the first two years, which was good because I had to compensate for the lost time and bad grades! Nevertheless, I completed my studies and achieved my Bachelor of Arts in Intermediate Education. I had earned my degree, but getting a teaching job in Raleigh, North Carolina, proved challenging. I had difficulty finding employment, and it weighed heavily on me.

I was blind in this state of my mind. I did not know it then, but I know now that the Lord was tugging at my heartstrings about my lifestyle. My outward woman looked like a picture of success, but my inner man was in turmoil. Before God opened this door of favor to me, I got tired of the way I was living. It was so much that I contemplated suicide. I saw myself as an unfilled, worthless individual. I wanted to be accepted; however, I felt constantly rejected. The pressure of life and my ridiculous choices caught up with me.

My mother called me one day and told me she wanted me to come home. I had heard they needed teachers in Pamlico County School system, but I was a bit skeptical. Nevertheless, I applied for a teaching position with that school system and Craven County Schools. As time would have it, I received a call from Craven County Schools to come in for an interview. The job was in Havelock, North Carolina. It was an assistant reading teacher position, working with "English as a second language" (ESL) students.

These ESL students were from Japan, Vietnam, and other foreign countries. Some were illiterate in English, but a few could speak the language in moderation. I soon found out that I had my job cut out for me. The challenge was intense; however, I was willing and available to learn. After six months of probation, they offered me a regular teacher position within the school system.

The truth is the Lord's grace, love, and favor were being extended to me while I was yet in my sinful state. Proverbs 8:35 (ESV) teaches us that "whoever finds me [wisdom] finds life, and obtains favor from the Lord." These small steps of faith—yielding and following after wisdom, being willing and available to learn—provided an intersection point in my life. God knew it was time for transition and presented me with the opportunity. It was up to me to make the most of that opportunity.

Life is not always simple, but when the wind of the Holy Spirit is blowing, even a carnal unsaved fool should be able to sense it is God moving on your behalf. It did not take a rocket scientist to tell me that God was speaking to my destiny. God had His mighty hand on me, and although I had had previous thoughts of suicide, I knew someone was praying for me, which helped me through that dark and challenging place.

Many of you may be dealing with the same issues. Yet, the Lord's junctions or intersections are an inflection point to help bring about a transition in all our lives. When we humble ourselves, we will begin to see the Light shining in our path. Even though this meant I would return home, I humbled myself and took the plunge. And God met me in my humble obedience.

Chapter 2
How Did I Get Here?

Despite all the accolades and accomplishments, I wondered and questioned who I was. Looking back, I had a problem with my identity because of an inferiority complex that haunted me for as long as I could remember. Unknowingly, we often fail to account for our wounds (as well as the effects that others' wounds have on our lives), not realizing that the buried emotions will become the root causes of future harmful behavior patterns and emotional breakdowns. No matter what I achieved, I did not feel like I was good enough to accomplish the call of God in my life. Looking at it now, I spent much wasted time comparing myself to others believing and thinking I was inadequate. It is strange to see everything good about someone else and see yourself as dung (garbage/waste).

I had insecurities, a vast perceived lack of worth, and very low self-esteem. I suppressed the abuse I went through as a young child, which caused me to smother my emotional healing. These wrong mindsets had been formed at an early age, along with a deeply rooted sense of rejection from my childhood experiences. I was forced to close my spirit and mind to the truth. It caused me to believe that it was okay to be treated the way I was. The protection I needed from the adults around me was not expressed. Instead, I suffered pain and neglect; I was used as a child laborer to care for babies when I was barely an adolescent.

I grew up believing that my father had rejected me. I later discovered that it was because of his insecurities and fear of harming me (as a daughter) based on his first cousin harming (molesting) his daughter. His fears caused him to isolate himself from me. But all I knew then was that his fatherly love was lacking in my life. I ached inside to have that validation and love from him. Experiencing rejection on this level caused me to think that I was unlovable and that something was wrong with me. I did not think I was pretty, smart, or good enough. I compared myself to my brother because he was always with my dad; therefore, I constantly struggled to compete for my father's affection and love.

It was not until one of my cousins from New York visited us and shared the message of redemption and salvation with me that I began to question my purpose and reason for existing. I had many doubts about religion, different gods, and why we need to receive Jesus only for salvation. She invited the family to attend church with her during her visit before returning to New York the next morning. I was skeptical, but I went to church with them that morning.

I had no idea that her visit would be a pivotal turning point in my life and in finding answers to those doubts. I turned my attention to the message during the service, and the truth reached my heart. It was the fourth Sunday of January 1977. I received the Lord Jesus Christ as my Savior. I knew I was saved and born again; however, I had much to learn about my new life in Christ. I did not yet realize all that would happen within me, but I knew my life was different. Everything seemed brand new. The sun was brighter, the air smelled fresher, and God's creation was more noticeable than ever. I even experienced compassion for the dead animals hit and left dead on the highway. ***God's grace changed me from the inside out.***

I began to attend Bible study and prayer services. I acquainted myself with other young members of the church. I developed strong, wholesome relationships with believers of like-faith, which helped me grow spiritually. This process would begin with a visit to the potter's house.

As my prayer life expanded, I developed an intimate relationship with Jesus. The Lord began to reveal Himself in ways I could not explain or understand. I knew I was different, and my desires immediately changed.

> Therefore if any man be in Christ, he is a new creature: old things have passed away; behold, all things have become new. (2 Corinthians 5:17)

> For Jehovah God is our Light and our Protector. He gives us grace and glory. No good

thing will he withhold from those who walk
along his paths. (Psalm 84:11 TLB)

As strange as it may seem, I had become comfortable portraying a façade to cover my painful identity. Have you experienced that? Most of humanity (if not all) has "hidden" issues. Many of these may have been suppressed so deeply in our souls that we refuse to acknowledge they exist, let alone have the courage to deal with them. We often continue to function in life as if nothing ever happened. We tend to walk through life wearing masks to cover our pain. We shield our painful identities because we have not yet received our true identity in Christ.

But thank God! The Holy Spirit will use circumstances in our lives to bring about the development needed. Through the work of the Holy Spirit, we can begin to understand that our old identity came from the issues we were exposed to. But! The new identity comes from God and is pure, whole, worthy, and undefiled!

The Lord wants us to hear His voice. His voice is *the voice of truth*. God is always speaking to us, even when we are attempting to suppress His voice or make excuses for our faults. The Father is just waiting for us to surrender to His purposes. His Word has creative power, and He knows how to bring about the desired consequences for our lives.

Let's think about the example in the Bible in Genesis 3:8. When the Lord came to Adam and Eve in the garden, they heard the voice of the Lord God walking in the garden in the cool of the day, as they had many times before. *But this time*, they both hid from the presence of the Lord God among the garden's trees. Why would they hide from God? Because they, for the first time, were hearing *the voice of human reasoning* inside them instead of the voice of truth.

Psychology will tell you that "reasoning is used not only when we want to solve an immediate problem but also when we anticipate future problems. Reasoning plays a significant role in one's adjustment to the environment. It not only determines one's cognitive activities but also influences the behavior and personality."[1]

At first, reasoning *seems good* and logical. But we must realize that *human reasonings first appeared when separation from God resulted from sin*. And just like that first time in the garden, when we fail to take time to think about the outcome of our choices, it may lead to terrible consequences. Like Adam and Eve, we (humanity) often try to hide or blame others for our poor decisions.

The voice of reasoning will always cause us to operate in the natural, carnal realm. That is the realm of our flesh. The flesh of an unregenerated person retains fear, doubt, unbelief, and pride. These negative traits will cause one to be illogical and think in ways inconsistent with one's new nature in Christ.

These expressions might sound like, "You are okay; you do not need God." Or, "You can make it on your own." Perhaps you hear, "You don't need anyone, especially not God." Or even, "You are not good enough. You won't be accepted.

You should hide who you really are." This voice of foolishness will keep you wondering for years, trying to figure out your destiny.

But the voice of truth, the voice of our gracious Heavenly Father, regularly calls us to come to Him! We will be forever lost until we yield and humble ourselves before His presence. Humbling ourselves is an encounter everyone in our Father's Kingdom should practice. No matter what your position, status, and title may be in this life, we all will be required to answer the summoning of our Lord as He calls unto us…

> Come to Me, all you who labor and are heavy-laden and overburdened, and I will cause you to rest. [I will ease and relieve and refresh your souls.]
>
> Take My yoke upon you and learn of Me, for I am gentle (meek) and humble (lowly) in heart, and you will find rest (relief and ease and refreshment and recreation and blessed quiet) for your souls.
>
> For My yoke is wholesome (useful, good—not harsh, hard, sharp, or pressing, but comfortable, gracious, and pleasant), and My burden is light and easy to be borne. (Matthew 11:28–30 AMPC)

Jesus wants us to get acquainted with the Father. We are His children who have been running and hiding long enough from our Father. It is high time to get acquainted with true spiritual life and the one Who is Life and who you are.

Chapter 3
Our True Value

I did not know who I was through many years, tears, and heartbreaks in life. Since I did not know my worth or value, it was challenging to believe I was worthy of anything. My major connections and acquaintances were with my family, my job, and my relationships with my friends.

Perhaps one of the most painful stages of life is not knowing who you are and not understanding where you are at the level of your development. It is like looking into a mirror; when you walk away, you forget what you looked like. In the Bible, James 1:24 says, "for he beholds himself, and then goeth his way and straightway forgetteth what manner of man he was."

Getting acquainted with our true value is the beginning of the learning and growing process. The dictionary tells us that *acquainted* refers to a person known to one to be well-informed but usually not a confidant. It requires experiencing and taking the time to know an individual.[2] It is part of our growth and development.

The first stage[3] of my spiritual growth is the **nepios** phase. This Greek word is pronounced **nay'-pee-os**.[4] It is defined as an infant, a simple-minded or immature person, unlearned and unenlightened. As a believer, we must recognize and be able to identify where we are in our development in Christ Jesus. When we get saved, we are not birthed into the Kingdom of God fully grown like Adam and Eve. I know I have been made complete in Jesus in His Kingdom. That's a legal position for all true sons of God. Yet, just as a child in the natural must grow and learn, so it is in the Kingdom. We must grow and mature spiritually—in our identity, in our relationship with Christ, and in our relationships with others.

Jesus desires to call us to Himself and place His yoke upon us so that we learn of Him (Matthew 11:29). We will go through many seasons of growth while reaching our destiny. I never had a problem learning. So, when Jesus said to take His yoke, I knew I would have to go after Him with everything He had already provided for me. *Take* is an action verb; therefore, I had to be willing to align the spirit of my mind in harmony with His Word and to learn all I needed to know about my Lord. I had to do this intentionally.

During the process, I looked intensely into the word *yoke*. Why? Because I was hungry! Understand this beloved one, a yoke is an implement to keep two animals flowing together when pulling a heavy load. Let's say that the animals stay connected to the yoke. In that case, the person maneuvering the implement will have control of the animals in the yoke. The burden of the load will be easy for the animals to pull if they stay connected, aligning themselves to the yoke. That remains true for us when we are yoked to Jesus.

Part of the yoke, and of learning of Him, was developing my relationship with Jesus, The Word of God. That came and still comes through studying the Word. The true growth process began with becoming familiar with Him and becoming His disciple. By staying yoked and connected to the Living Word, we allow the Holy Spirit to train and equip us for life. His ways are easy. My task is to study and learn about my Heavenly Father. He loved me so much that He would give His Son just for me.

Learning to submit, to be subject to the Holy Spirit, was a humbling experience for me. It is for most people. When we think of our agenda, ambitions, and what we deem more important than His plans, it is easy to operate in a spirit of idolatry. But those things are rubbish outside of Christ. Our teacher, The Holy Spirit, intentionally teaches us about God's agenda. His agenda, desires, and priorities are the most important in our walk with Christ.

One of the most important things I've learned is that God always wanted a family that would be in harmony with Him. Ephesians 1:4 (NIV) tells us:

> For he chose us in him before the creation of the world to be holy and blameless in his sight. In love he predestined us for adoption to sonship through Jesus Christ, in accordance with his pleasure and will.

Scarcely did we know anything about the experiences the Lord prepared for us before our destinies were revealed. Jesus was getting me ready to be introduced to His divine presence. He wanted me well informed about His glory and to seek Him intimately. It is very simple. He wanted me to see myself as He sees me.

This shy, timid, stammering speaking woman was about to take her journey in life, discovering things about herself that she could never dream possible. The Lord expects every one of us to experience this journey. He wants us to experience the deepest innermost depths of His presence, unlike anything we have ever known.

I was amazed to discover that God has a sense of humor. And He uses the natural things of the world as an analogy to show what He is doing within us spiritually. For example, in my own journey, He showed me that my development process in the teaching profession was much like a visit to a potter's house! He said, "I want you to use the analogy of a visit to the potter's house. It will help you to understand your spiritual development in my Kingdom."

How is that? *Life is about being taught.* It is about learning and submitting to someone greater than yourself. It is about being willing to put your life in the hands of others, who will be used to help develop you from the inside out.

One discovers that development takes time in the potter's house. The instruments God will use to construct our lives are chosen by Him. Why? Since He is the Potter, everything He has for the blueprint of our lives will require all the tools

He will use to complete His desired results. We will not, at first, understand the process. There will be many questions we will ask on the way. We will make many mistakes and fall now and then; however, the Potter will be there to pick us up.

For example, I did not have a close relationship with my earthy father. Before he died, he shared his reasons for rejecting me. Sharing his reasons for rejecting me did not heal my brokenness, but I was able to forgive him. This was growth for me.

I was getting acquainted with who I am through my Father's love. He wants me to learn to be a citizen of His heavenly Kingdom. This will be done without fear, doubt, or any other dysfunction. Now I can see why he wanted me to understand my Father's love.

You may ask these questions: How can we have a relationship with someone we cannot see? How can we become a disciple? Why is it important for us to become a servant? How will I learn about His love? What is my destiny? What is my assignment in His Kingdom? Since we are His children, all these answers are found in developing a relationship with the one who has created us, Our Potter, Father God.

We must know who we are, our real worth, and our value. We must come to the purest level (the very essence of submission) of placing our lives in the hands of Jesus. We must discover Him, learn of His love for us, understand His Kingdom, and, most importantly, realize why He chooses us.

Chapter 4

The Potter's House

Many of us are constantly bombarded with the lack of a father in the home or our lives. My father was an absentee dad. Sure, he worked outside the home and provided most of our basic needs. But on the weekend, he would run the street. Most of the time, my brother David had an opportunity to spend quality time with him. I loathed that because I wanted my time with him too. There was no father/daughter closeness or communication. If you would ask me, "What do you know about your father?" The only thing I could share with you is, "He is my dad, and he goes to work and spends most of his time doing other things outside the home."

He was strict when it came to discipline. In other words, he needed more time for me. Many of us suffer from a lack of affirmation from our Father. I did not know what having a father's love was like. It is one thing to experience rejection; however, abandonment of the heart is another issue altogether. The lack of a father-daughter relationship caused me to search for love in all the wrong places. I began getting involved with people but found they were unconcerned about me or my emotions.

Looking back on my early life, I learned that what a father may deem important in his life is not necessarily important to the family. In my father's case, he had no prior knowledge or vantage point of being a father. I can say one wonderful thing about my dad: he loved to work. He wanted to make sure he had something that would represent his achievements. Most fathers can be extremely competitive. Some fathers may get involved in sports, some outside hobbies, or work on projects from home. However, when they are deeply involved in their own pursuits, everything else can become second fiddle.

My daddy loved Cadillacs. His income did not necessarily warrant him being able to afford one; nevertheless, that is what he loved, and that is what he bought. Daddy had to keep up the appearance or an image of a man of wealth. However, he had the nerve to put a sign on the front of the car with a license tag that read, "Poor Boy." What an irony!

He was known as the street *lover boy*. He was unfaithful to my mom. How do I know? I witnessed him cheating on her on one of his escapades. On one occasion, I thought he was taking me out for a father-daughter outing. Instead, he picked up his girlfriend. I was around seven or eight years old. He told me not to tell my mother because it would make her angry. Wow!! I did not know what to do or what to expect. All I knew, I had to keep my mouth shut and function as if everything was all right. But, I do understand that my mother was not a saint either. There were things she did as

28

well. And to this day, she does not know that at the ripe age of four, I saw and remember what she did secretly.

Now, certainly, everyone has a past; many have family members with skeletons in their closets. We must learn that these skeletons will influence our behavior if we do not deal with them. If they are not dealt with, it will leave you emotionally scarred. And, because of those scars, we often try to *fit in* and constantly lose a piece of ourselves in the trying process. The word *fit* bears reference to being the right size or shape for someone or something.[5] We spend needless time searching for our identity in places, with superficial things, and with people, not realizing what is missing is the broken relationship we never experienced with our fathers or mother. Therefore, much of our heartache, brokenness, or behaviors result from deep wounds of rejection.

It does not take long in life to realize that people, even the closest friends or relatives, have personal issues and will disappoint us. I have learned from conversations and experience that this happens to most people as we go through life, choosing those we tend to hang around. I kept many things (like these above) deeply suppressed in my soul, which eventually surfaced in my own behaviors.

> When my father and mother forsake me, then
> the Lord will take me up. (Psalm 27:10)

Perhaps many of you may have been forsaken by your fathers or mothers in the sense that I am sharing. You know, many parents do not realize the extent of their imprint on the souls of their children. Leading and disciplining the children is important, especially *how* they are led. We must realize that our parents are humans, and, just like us, they are seriously flawed without Jesus.

As I contemplated the relationships of fathers and/or mothers with their children and the wounds that sometimes occur from those relationships, Holy Spirit began to deal with me about developing a message entitled, "A Visit to the Potter's House." Actually, the Lord instructed me to conduct this mission years ago, and I failed to obey Him until eventually God gave it to me as a message to preach at a conference. Although I did not know this when I began to study about the potter and his work, my own deeply suppressed events and feelings were among the things that were healed as I obeyed His leading.

As I began to study about the potter, I had no idea that the natural information I learned about his work and ways would bring such revelation to enlighten me. In retrospect, I also could not have imagined then the impact it would have on my healing and even further, that it would revisit me in this season of my life and ultimately become this book! But, having grown much over my lifetime, I see clearly now that God the Father has a unique purpose for me in His Kingdom at this time, and obedience to Him is my utmost priority in life.

As I present those revelations in this book, I also trust it will greatly help many of you. As we look into the life of a potter, in the pages of this book and for our illustrations, for clarity, the capitalized proper name *Potter* or *Master Potter* will be used to refer to the Holy Father (the Lord) in the analogy and observation. When speaking in general of pottery making professionals, you will notice a lower case for the common noun *potter*—except at the beginning of sentences or in titles, of course.

Facts I Learned About The Potter:

Some potters make vessels as a hobby, but others have chosen this as a career. Many potters are self-employed and can usually set their own hours. Typically, self-employed pottery makers have an art studio where they work. The pottery studio helps ensure that concentration on the masterpiece is uninterrupted. Potters must have a safe and spacious place to create and complete their work without distractions or interludes.

Their income typically comes from selling their works to individuals via art galleries, craft fairs, or personal studio showrooms, and some sell their wares online. Besides self-employment, there are other employment options. Many potters work as instructors, teaching pottery-making classes and workshops in schools, colleges, or private settings. Many craft artists teach art to others. To teach art in an elementary or secondary school, an individual must usually have a teaching certificate and a bachelor's degree. Teaching at a college or university level requires an advanced degree in fine arts. Some work for private sector industries, like pottery manufacturers. However, those with formal education might also work in art galleries, museums, and foundations.

The working of the potter's livelihood is called *potting*. The potter must have clay to do this work. He must choose clay (not just any dirt or mud) to shape the desired piece. The potter's original purpose is to take a piece of clay and turn it into a useful object.

There are five broad phases of the potter's job: *chiseling* (to choose and dig up the raw clay with a clay chisel—a spade-like digging tool); *prepare* (a long process of drying it out, cleansing and watering, and reforming the clay); *conditioning* the clay; *shaping and smoothing*; and finally, three steps in the *firing* of the clay.

All of these phases are worked through in order and over time by the potter to produce the desired end result. We will discuss each of these phases in the coming chapters. If I can simply explain as an introduction, the potter must not only select the clay, but the potter must also remove stones, debris, or other impurities before he can shape the vessel into the finished work.

The potter raises and shapes the prepared clay on a revolving wheel, using hands, fingers, and thumbs. The potter shapes and smooths the surfaces of finished pieces using rubber scrapers and a wet sponge. Every tool the potter uses is for the benefit and purpose of developing, forming, molding, and shaping the kind of vessel he has in mind.[6]

The work of the potter is an ongoing process. He consistently works hard to accomplish his task. Naturally, the clay does not know what is going on with its substance; however, it must remain fixed in the hand of the potter. **The mind of the potter holds the finished product while his hands move the clay toward that finished work.**

A potter often makes dishes, plates, and other objects from the prepared clay. The Bible indicates that clay was widely used in the Old Testament for making bricks, mortar, and pottery. Exactly like a potter chooses his clay with the end vessel in mind, in that imagery, we can see that our Master Potter, Jesus, deliberately and intentionally chose us from this world and the foolish things to confound the wise. He chose the low-born, the insignificant, and purposed them to use for His pleasure.

> The word which came to Jeremiah from the Lord, saying, "Arise, and go down to the potter's house, and there I will cause thee to hear my words."

> Then I went down to the potter's house, and, behold, he wrought a work on the wheels. And the vessel that he made of clay was marred in the hand of the potter: so he made it again another vessel, as seemed good to the potter to make it.

> Then the word of the Lord came to me, saying, "O house of Israel, cannot I do with you

as this potter?" saith the Lord. "Behold, as the clay is in the potter's hand, so are ye in mine hand, O house of Israel.

At what instant I shall speak concerning a nation, and concerning a kingdom, to pluck up, and to pull down, and to destroy it; If that nation, against whom I have pronounced, turn from their evil, I will repent of the evil that I thought to do unto them.

And at what instant I shall speak concerning a nation, and concerning a kingdom, to build and to plant it; If it do evil in my sight, that it obey not my voice, then I will repent of the good, wherewith I said I would benefit them.

Now therefore go to, speak to the men of Judah, and to the inhabitants of Jerusalem, saying, 'Thus saith the Lord; "Behold, I frame evil against you, and devise a device against you: return ye now every one from his evil way, and make your ways and your doings good."'

And they said, "There is no hope: but we will walk after our own devices, and we will every one do the imagination of his evil heart." (Jeremiah 18:1–12)

The Heavenly Father wants all of us to embrace Him as our Father. He desires to bless us, heal us, and welcome us as Loving Father. Let's put all of this into the context of our pottery analogy. Our Master Potter offers the loving hand to reshape, smooth, and remake us, a vessel free from scars or marring. Like us, the clay did not have a choice about who its potter was. None of us chose the family we began in. And, most likely, you also had very little say in whether they chose evil or good. Because many of us have suffered rejection and abandonment from one or both of our parents, what often happens is that we presume He is the same as our earthly father (or other influence) is or was.

The good news is, regardless of their choices, and just as the potter chose the clay without giving it a say in its existence, we were chosen by God the Father, our Potter and Creator, to be smoothed and shaped into beautiful vessels *in the Maker's hands.*

It was easy for me to receive Jesus as my Savior—with my life's wounds, hurts, and disappointments, I knew that I wanted and needed saving! However, I found it was more difficult for me to see God as **Father**. It hurt to think about the rejection that I went through with my dad. My dad needed to understand what was important about taking care of the immediate needs of family affairs. In his weakness, he did not have a vision for the family. He was shortsighted and concerned with his selfish needs. He loved cars, women, and money. And as a result, I did not experience the fatherly love and affection a daughter needed. He failed to mold, shape, and develop a trusting connection with me. The very thing he did not want to happen to me happened. He was not there to protect and counsel me through my issues. I kept all these things shut up inside.

It also took me a long time to be comfortable around other leaders. It was because I saw them much like my earthly father. I learned as I matured in Christ that we should never judge others from the former relationships we were exposed to. This is a common issue that many if not most people struggle with. For example:

Have you been suppressing the pain and superimposing bitterness from within onto your life and people in it?

Are you are walking around today with pent-up hostility, brokenness, unforgiveness, inferiority, and poor self-esteem?

Do you find that you will use every excuse in the book to deny the factual issues destroying your life and your relationship with others?

I have been there. I can relate. That is how I can tell you with certainty that there is a journey of healing and reformation for each of us. When I was impressed by Holy Spirit to visit (to study out) the message of and lessons in the potter's house, I began to see and experience the fullness of God (Father, Son, and Holy Spirit) as the true *Master Potter.* And in that, I found great healing.

The Lord told me I could no longer hold or blame my father for his inadequacies. My dad's inability to relate as a father was passed down to him by his father. Dad was never taught how to be a father; therefore, he could not give me something he did not possess, that which he had no knowledge of.

I knew I had to face my wounds, to face the demons that tormented me. I knew it would be a journey, but I was ready to take it. First, I had to allow the Holy Spirit to become my teacher, showing me the true nature of God. I had to trust in the discipline of the Holy Spirit by renewing my mind in the Word of God. And most of all, I needed to purposefully develop an intimate relationship with Jesus, the living expression of the Master Potter.

Chapter 5

The Master Potter

It is the will of the Father for us to begin to know Him, our Master Potter, and to learn to flow with and in the mind of Christ. Our humble submission to and communion with Him will cause us to be stable when hardship, fear, circumstances, and problems appear. We were never an afterthought in our Father's Kingdom when he called and birthed us into existence. It was for His divine purpose; His great love for His creation caused him to do what He did.

The next step in the process is yielding *in the Maker's hands*, learning to have an intimate relationship with the Godhead through relationship with Jesus. True commitment, discipline, and obedience will be required. This will allow us to understand our sonship with the Father. Author Hubert A Morris wrote on this in the book, *Jesus and His Covenant*:

[In the Supreme Spirit Being,] there was the divine wisdom of all knowledge, understanding, and insight (omniscience). He knew that there would be a creation of all things. In doing so, He knew He had to establish a means, or medium, for the communication between the creator and the created. The communicating medium would, of necessity, have to be so related to the created that there would be perfect harmony between all concerned.

Therefore, the Supreme Spirit Being formed and fashioned of Himself, the Expression Person of the Godhead: The Logos, called the Word.[7]

Jesus is the Word, the Logos, and the Express Image of the Godhead, the Father.

In the beginning was the Word, and the Word was with God, and the Word was God. He was with God in the beginning. Through him, all things were made; without him, nothing was made that has been made. In him was life, and that life was the light of all mankind. (John 1:1–4 NIV)

When I received Jesus as my savior, I received everything I needed from the Godhead. My relationship with Jesus was the Father's plan from the foundation of the world. Having a relationship and understanding of who Jesus is, was an intentional setup for me to learn about my true Father. We discovered in John 14:7–9 (NIV), Jesus spoke to the disciples about this powerful truth:

> If you really know me, you will know my Father as well. From now on, you do know him and have seen him.
>
> Philip replied, "Lord, show us the Father, and that will be enough for us."
>
> Jesus answered: "Don't you know me, Philip, even after I have been among you such a long time? Anyone who has seen me has seen the Father. How can you say, 'Show us the Father?'"

Jesus, the express image of Father God, my pattern as a son of God (Hebrews 1:3), initiated my deliverance and healing process. I needed confidence in Him to understand and learn who my Father was. As the Father developed a loving, trusting relationship with me through Jesus, He knew I could also embrace my Loving Father. His thoughts were always about making me whole; however, He had to set the right environment for me to experience completeness. Jesus told his disciples, *"If you have seen or experienced me, you have beheld the very essence of your Father."* I realized I was a flawed vessel, but I was still on His mind and *in the Maker's hands!*

So in studying, we can see that the potter's house is an analogy to the Kingdom of God. The principle of the Kingdom is entering His way. The question may be, how do we enter the Kingdom? Our Father reveals His ways, thoughts, and doings in the lifestyle of the King operating in His Kingdom. Our Lord is not asking us to live any differently than He lives. The more we yield ourselves to the Spirit, He will reveal and show us how to live the Kingdom lifestyle. In essence, we become more Christ-like. As He was on the earth, so shall we become; the key is the becoming aspect. We are the direct image or manifestation of Him *now,* representing Him as believers.

The Master Potter is a creator, a planner, a builder, and an engineer. Everything He does is strategically planned for His work. When a natural potter thinks about making a vessel, he carefully chooses the position, location, and environment to create and develop his work. Our heavenly Father, the Master Potter, purposefully chose a location. He strategically chose a safe and spacious place to perform His work. He could not and did not allow distractions to keep Him from making His intended creation. Genesis 1:26 shows us that the Father was not working alone but that the Trinity was in unison, completing the work of creation. Our Lord had access to this vast universe to create everything He wanted. Before doing it, He surveyed the stratosphere. Jesus wanted to make sure everything was fit and ready for use. By His spoken Word, He caused it to come to fruition. He manifested everything by His spoken Word.

> By the word of the Lord, the heavens were
> made, and by the breath of his mouth, all
> their host. (Psalm 33:6 ESV)

We can see in Genesis 1:1–25, that the heavens were formed, and the waters of the deep were established. Everything complied with the spoken Word when He hovered or brooded over the entire domain. The Father ensured that everything He made was connected and adapted before making his next move. We can look around even now and observe His confidence and consideration in creating! God wanted to ensure everything would be suitable for and adaptable to man.

But when He was ready to create man, God chose to form him by Hand. The Lord is the creator of everything; he engineered everything according to His divine specification. The Bible says in Genesis 2:7 (ESV; emphasis added):

> Then the Lord God formed the man of ***dust***
> from the ground and breathed into his nos-
> trils the breath of life, and the man became a
> living creature.

Strong's Concordance lists the word ***dust*** as used in the scripture above as the Hebrew word ***âphâr*** (aw-fawr') from Strong's H6080: dust (as powdered or gray); hence, clay, earth, mud:—ashes, dust, earth, ground, mortar, powder.[8] The main difference between clay and ordinary mud is that clay is a soft rock-based compound often used for sculpting. Mud is a mixture of water and a combination of soil, silt, and clay.[9] We will see this substance as we study the potting process in the next few chapters. To briefly explain, the dry dust occurs after the Potter has chiseled the desired portion of clay and allowed time and weathering to reduce it to bone dry dust. Then He begins to reconstitute it into pliable material, clay, which can be shaped, smoothed, and molded. *Selah*. (Stop and think on that!)

When God chose Adam, He wanted the right material to sculpt and mold him; when He did, He called the human *Adam*. Adam was formed by God and made in perfection; Adam had no flaws. When God breathed life into his nostrils, he became a living soul. God gave Adam a name and gave him a job. He gave him dominion to reign and rule.

In an article for The Israel Institute of Biblical Studies, Hebrew scholar Julia Blum writes:

> Another amazing connection that we find in this chapter [referring to Genesis 2] is the connection between Adam and Adamah – the ground, the land, the soil. We commented previously on this when we spoke about Adam's name; while this connection is lost completely in translation, in Hebrew, it just stands out; we clearly hear the word adamah in the word Adam. You may remember different explanations I shared with you then –

and in particular, a beautiful midrashic comment: 'Man (Adam) and the land or ground (Adamah) share the name because they were both created in a basic status requiring cultivation in order to reach their greatest potential—to bring forth fruit.'"[10]

The earth, the vessels, and everything in this domain were originally in the mind of our Lord.

> Yours, O Lord, is the greatness and the power and the glory and the victory and the majesty, for all that is in the heavens and in the earth, is yours. Yours is the Kingdom, O Lord, and you are exalted as head above all. Both riches and honor come from you, and you rule over all. In your hand are power and might, and in your hand it is to make great and to give strength to all. (1 Chronicles 29:11–12 ESV)

> "For all these things My hand has made, so all these things came into being [by and for Me]," declares the Lord. "But to this one, I will look [graciously], To him who is humble and contrite in spirit, and who [reverently] trembles at My word and honors My commands." (Isaiah 66:2 AMP)

When speaking of God, the Father, Jesus the Son, and The Holy Spirit, although they are three unique expressions, we know from the Bible that they are One. The mind of God (Supreme Spirit Being), who is the originator, understands the purpose of His creation. We are His creation chosen for a specified purpose in His Kingdom. As Elohim, our three-in-One God, He is the Creator. All of these scriptures (and others) point us to the divine intention of the heart of God:

> In the beginning, God created the heaven and the earth. (Genesis 1:1)

> He stretcheth out the north over the empty place, and hangeth the earth upon nothing. (Job 26:7)

> Of old hast thou laid the foundation of the earth: and the heavens are the work of thy hands. (Psalms 102:25)

> For even if there are so-called gods, whether in heaven or on earth (as indeed there are many "gods" and many "lords"), yet for us there is but one God, the Father, from whom all things came and for whom we live; and there is but one Lord, Jesus Christ, through whom all things came and through whom we live. (1 Corinthians 8:5–6 NIV)

> Through faith we understand that the worlds
> were framed by the word of God, so that
> things which are seen were not made of things
> which do appear. (Hebrews 11:3)

From the choosing process, framing process, and speaking process, the Father's consideration and planning were done in advance. Nothing was an addendum; nothing was by happenstance or an accident. Everything was done deliberately from the will and the mind of God. Paul wrote,

> And he said, "The God of our fathers appointed you to know his will, to see the Righteous One and to hear a voice from his mouth;" (Acts 22:14 ESV)

> Not many of you were wise according to worldly standards, not many were powerful, not many were of noble birth. But God chose what is foolish in the world to shame the wise; God chose what is weak in the world to shame the strong; God chose what is low and despised in the world, even things that are not, to bring to nothing things that are, so that no human being might boast in the presence of God. (1 Corinthians 1:26–29 ESV)

Jesus, as the Master Potter, saw and foreknew what His desires and intentions were for our destiny. We may struggle with knowing who we are and what to do in certain seasons of our lives. In our confusion, we find ourselves going ahead of the Lord, making decisions on our own. Ignorance causes us to become anxious and impatient, and it causes us to get in trouble. Well, what do we do? Typically, we resort to human efforts and counsel to direct us in our lives. We must resist doing that and return to the Word, trusting that Jesus knows what is best for our lives.

There are many things the Lord does not want in His Kingdom. Falseness is one of those things. The Lord is Truth. We are made in His image. So we can know that He doesn't desire us to be an impostor, a pretender, an imitator, or a trickster. Let's look at each of these identities.

An impostor is a person that assumes a false identity or title for the purpose of deception;[11] a pretender is a person that pretends: such as one who lays claim to something, like a claimant to a throne who is held to have no just title or one who makes a false or hypocritical show;[12] an imitator is a person who mimics or copies the behavior or actions of another.[13] A trickster is a person who cheats or deceives people to get ahead.[14] It is possible to assume the role of any of these identities when we do not know who we are in our purpose or do not have a personal relationship with Jesus.

> For many deceivers [heretics posing as Christians] have gone out into the world, those

who do not acknowledge and confess the coming of Jesus Christ in the flesh (bodily form). This [person, the kind who does this] is the deceiver and the anti-christ [that is, the antagonist of Christ].

Watch yourselves so that you do not lose what we have accomplished together but that you may receive a full and perfect reward [when He grants rewards to faithful believers]. Anyone who runs on ahead and does not remain in the doctrine of Christ [that is, one who is not content with what He taught] does not have God; but the one who continues to remain in the teaching [of Christ does have God], he has both the Father and the Son.

If anyone comes to you and does not bring this teaching [but diminishes or adds to the doctrine of Christ], do not receive or welcome him into your house, and do not give him a greeting or any encouragement; for the one who gives him a greeting [who encourages him or wishes him success, unwittingly] participates in his evil deeds. (2 John 7–11 AMP)

Knowing who Jesus is and receiving Him as Lord and controller of our lives will keep us grounded and rooted in grace. We must continue and remain in His Word, stay humble, know who we are in Christ Jesus, and love ourselves and others. We do not have to aspire for positions and titles. Our place, setting, and position have already been established in Jesus our Lord, the Potter. Therefore, we do not have to be concerned about being an impostor, an imitator, a pretender, or a trickster, because we faithfully understand who Jesus is in our lives.

Whom Does Jesus Need In His Kingdom?

We are God's Royal Priesthood company; we have been selected and trained in God's school of sonship dominion to restore all creation to God. Of these King-Priests, it is written,

> ...Thou hast redeemed us to God by Thy blood out of every kindred, and tongue, and people, and nation; and hast made us unto our God kings and priests: and we shall reign on the earth. (Revelation 5:9–10)

This is a season when Father God desires all his sons and daughters to know who they are in the Kingdom. Many broken individuals are like broken vessels discarded in the potter's field. Jesus has already made a place available for all who will believe His word, trust in Him (and therefore the

Father), and receive all that has been given for them to exist in the Kingdom. His Word has residence within us. Believing Him has given us full authority to know who we are in the kingdom. Our connection and understanding of who we are to the Father give us all the right to experience everything on this earth as it is in heaven.

He expects us to believe in Him as our deliverer, savior, and healer and know that we are joint heirs with Jesus Christ. He desires that we believe in the finished work He has already completed. We must believe in the complete finished work for our assignment and destiny. As He was on this earth, we must begin to function in the will and authority given of the Father. He wants us to function with Him now in our destiny. In Genesis 1:26–28,

> God said, "Let Us make man in our image, after our likeness: and let them have domin- ion over the fish of the sea, and over the fowl of the air, and over the cattle, and over all the earth, and over every creeping thing that creepeth upon the earth."

We will never be able to fulfill our destiny in the king- dom of God if we do not know or understand our identity with Him in the kingdom. The number one job of satan is to steal, kill, and destroy our identity. Our job is to submit to the molding of our Potter, our heavenly Father, and allow the forming process to continue until we fully mature in our destiny. When we refuse to yield to the Lord's preparation and grooming process, we struggle against His will. If we are not careful, we become impostors, tricksters, and pretenders because we are immature children. God knows what is in the heart of all His children. Therefore, we must become pliable as clay *in the Maker's hands*, yielding to the process.

Despite our position in God's Kingdom, what title we address ourselves to be in the eyes of others, and what others may say about us, we will never be greater than our Father. When we humbly submit, abandon, and empty ourselves of ourselves, we become meet for the Master's use, ready to be saturated by Holy Spirit. Jesus wants us to be imbued, inspired, and permeated in His Glory and completely soaked in His anointing. We must remember that we are the clay, and He is the Potter.

Chapter 6
Chiseling Raw Clay

As I began to develop in my prayer life, Holy Spirit began an inner work in me. I had no idea what He was beginning at the time. Nevertheless, I continued praying. I came to learn that He was *chiseling the raw materials.*

As a new convert, I had anger issues. I dealt with fear, intimidation, bitterness, and unforgiveness; I had trust issues and self-esteem concerns. These hidden things began to be exposed as I became acquainted with my real Father and continued coming to Kingdom truths. I was suffering from a lack of confidence and a spirit of worthlessness—just like the impurities in *raw but chosen* clay!

Despite how we got here, where we may have come from, who our parents are, and what our past may have been like, *we all have a past.* Jesus predestined us from the beginning of time and chose us because of His love for His creation. Man did not have anything to do with the decision of the Father. (Discover more in Ephesians 1:4–6.) We may not yet see ourselves as noble, wise, strong, or acceptable individuals; however, we can be encouraged and have hope because our

Father God is the Potter. He chose us from the gutter-most and placed us in His Kingdom. We moved to the uttermost to confound those who would never think of us as people with prestige, power, and potential to do anything! (Explore this thought more in 1 Corinthians 1:26–29.)

Facing The Demons That Torment You

So, continuing my story... the chiseling process meant that it was time for me to face my wounds and the demons that tormented me. I did not know what I was longing for. I did not understand what was going on in my life. Jesus delivered me from smoking, drinking, fornicating, poor self-esteem, insecurity, suicidal tendencies, and so much more.

Despite all these victories, I was suffering from a deficiency of love and was experiencing a spiritual drought. I was hungry for the need to be accepted. My cravings were for attention that I needed from my father. What my earthly father could not do, Jesus took care of it.

The Lord knew it was the appointed time for transition in my life. I did not understand that my suffering was a temporary experience for that season. Who would ever think that the Father, my Potter, could take a nobody like me and choose me to do His will? **I felt like dirt, dung, filth, and unworthy all my life.** I had thought about killing myself, as though that would be the best way to solve all the problems and nonsense in my life. Thankfully, just as I contemplated taking matters into my own hands, Jesus spoke to my life. And just in time!

When life deals with us in a matter-of-fact manner or when issues visit us, God intentionally prepares us to transition to the next level in our destiny. While that might sound glamorous, I was in for a rude awakening. Jesus was indeed about to take nothing (me) and make something out of my life. *This is very much like a potter chooses and chisels clay from the earth. He begins removing the impurities.*

Jesus spoke to my heart about serving others and taking my mind off of myself. His plans may only sometimes make sense; however, this would be a part of my transitional phase. (We should never see or consider serving others a raw deal during our trauma phase. It may look like we are being used, taken advantage of, left alone, and abandoned, but our destiny is securely *in the Maker's hands*.) He would use servitude to heal my wounded, bleeding soul.

The Holy Spirit said, "While facing the demons that torment you, you must be willing to empty yourself of yourself." He was speaking about my inner man. I may have looked like this quite easy-going young woman; however, I had a lot of hidden heart issues that needed to be dealt with. The challenges I was dealing with, even though they were not self-imposed, were real. I had to humble myself by admitting I had to face my inner hurts. I had suppressed my memory from the traumas I had gone through. The first issue I had to deal with was forgiving my father. The second thing I had to do was forgive my abuser. And finally, I had to forgive myself for what I did to others. You may have heard the saying, "Hurt people will hurt people." Well, out of ignorance, that is what

I was unintentionally doing. I hurt people and pushed them away from me.

I was four years in the Kingdom and yet I did not realize I still had issues I needed to deal with. Without a doubt, I knew God called me into ministry to preach. I struggled to believe He wanted to use me to share His Word with others. I knew I loved Him; however, I fought with my identity and being received by others. I especially had a fundamental problem confronting my general overseer. Finally, after the Holy Spirit got a hold of me, I went to my pastor and shared my experience. To my surprise, he said the Lord had prepared him to receive my call.

The Ministry of Helps and Servitude was my first step in my journey to *receiving* my deliverance. (Jesus paid the price for my deliverance, but I still needed to receive it and walk in it.) I went through training for the work of the ministry. I did many service works in the organization, which helped equip me for the call. However, what I really needed was ***discipleship training***. Unfortunately, this was not a set curriculum in our church; therefore, it was not part of the equipping processes.

Many of you may be in ministry, doing the work of God, helping others, but you never took the time to allow the Lord to deal with you and your inner issues. That makes people vulnerable to failures, meltdowns, bitterness, offense, and more. If you haven't discovered this yet, you will. In pottery terms, this is remaining in the greenware stage, fragile, not having passed through the fire, so the vessel is more susceptible to become *cracked pots* or vessels that get *bent out of shape*, so to speak.

After serving God and being discipled in the Word for many years now, I came to understand that we all must start from the beginning as newborn babes in the Kingdom of God. At this stage of development, every believer must begin by becoming a disciple of Jesus. We mustn't allow the circumstances of life to cause us to become bitter. Instead, we must embrace Jesus and let Him make us better. Growing in one's destiny and purpose must first and foremost start with discipleship in His Word. At this stage and season of our growth, the Holy Spirit will develop an intimate relationship with His children.

I thank Jesus for His grace. Even though this process was not taught in the church, the Lord has His way of ensuring that we will not skip any levels of development if we want His perfect will to be done in our lives. The Grace of Jesus has been given to us to make us completely whole from the inside out. He will not abandon us because His plans for us in His Kingdom are eternal. We must realize that God is still modeling and shaping our lives to bring us to maturity.

In the traditional method of making pottery, after the potter digs the raw clay, he will allow it to be exposed to the weather for a year. He does this to permit the clay to disintegrate, then turns it over and allows it to dry out for another year. This is the preparation process of ancient Greek pottery masters.[15] In the modern method, the clay is put in a machine to disintegrate and accelerate aging. This process may facilitate the mass production of products for less expense and yield a higher profit. But the truth is that there is no comparison in quality. This is so instructive to us in our process as well!

The Kingdom of our Lord does not work like this mechanically accelerated process; that is an artificial concept to bypass development. So then, how does this process work? First, we must acknowledge that we need to be delivered. In our expectations for greatness in the Kingdom of God, we must allow Him to complete the work of weathering us, maturing us for greater things. As stated in the book of Acts 20:24 (ESV),

> But I do not account my life of any value nor as precious to myself, if only I may finish my course and the ministry that I received from the Lord Jesus, to testify to the gospel of the grace of God.

We cannot provide evidence of the greatness of the Kingdom of God in any area of our lives if we have not yet been delivered or allowed Him to fully mature us as sons of God. You may need help accepting who you are. You may feel anger, hatred, and all kinds of emotional upheaval, yet you do not know why.

What is the missing link in our relationship with God and with others? It may be as simple as looking in the mirror at your reflection and asking yourself, *"Do I know who I am?"* This is when Holy Spirit calls you to His throne room to come closer so He can reveal Himself to you. The closer we draw to Him, we will see and experience His love. By doing so, He will reveal who we are even as we are yet in our unfinished soulish state.

> Let us then approach God's throne of grace with confidence, so that we may receive mercy and find grace to help us in our time of need. (Hebrews 4:16 NIV)

When He took me into His throne room, He began tenderly revealing to me the impurities in the clay—all the emotional scars of the soul realm that I had suppressed through the years. The revelation of what was exposed was so painful that I could only weep agonizingly. I realized my soul (mind, will, emotions, behavior patterns) needed to be deeply touched by God. You could say that He was chiseling (digging into) the raw clay and exposing to me the preparation process like the ancient pottery masters. *In the Maker's hands,* I realized that I needed to be healed from the inside, in my innermost parts of the soul.

Made In His Image

We are spiritual beings who possess a soul (mind, will, and emotion) and live in a physical body. We are tripartite beings in our nature, designed this way by God Himself.

> So God created man in his own image, in the
> image of God created he him; male and fe-
> male created he them. (Genesis 1:27)

Yes, we may be born again, but our soul must *possess* (lay hold of) the healing that Christ provides. At rebirth in Christ, our spirit man is completely whole, refreshed, and made brand new; however, our soul man is under construction, being renewed by the Word of God, and our bodies remain connected, although not yet fully glorified.

Our inner man, the soul, needs to be renewed daily. The Bible teaches us that we must be renewed in the spirit of our minds. Colossians 3:10 states that the born-again believer has "put on the new self, which is being renewed in knowledge in the image of its Creator" (NIV). We also see powerful truths about renewal in Romans 12:

> Do not conform to the pattern of this world,
> but be transformed by the renewing of your
> mind. Then you will be able to test and ap-
> prove what God's will is—his good, pleasing
> and perfect will. (v. 2, NIV)

The process is a humbling experience for every child of God. We must familiarize ourselves with the Word of God to the degree that it is all we want and need, and we cannot live without it. To the born-again believer, the Bible says we must grow up!

Therefore, rid yourselves of all malice and all deceit, hypocrisy, envy, and slander of every kind. *Like newborn babies, crave pure spiritual milk,* so that by it you may grow up in your salvation, now that you have tasted that the Lord is good. (1 Peter 2:1–3 NIV; emphasis added.)

Paul, the apostle, wrote, "But I, brothers, could not address you as spiritual people, but as people of the flesh, as *infants* in Christ" (1 Corinthians 3:1 ESV; emphasis added).

The word *infants* used in that scripture is translated from the Greek word *nēpios*. **Nēpios** is often translated as "child, infant, childish, or an infant or a babe in Christ."[16] Babies are immature and self-centered, but everyone begins there!

Experiencing Stages Of Spiritual Growth

The Holy Spirit knew it was time for me to get acquainted with Him at this growth stage. Every child of God must be discipled by mature spiritual leaders. There are tremendous things that could be vastly improved in the lives of undisciplined members of the Body of Christ if they would only **allow themselves to be discipled!** How do I know? *I was one of them.*

This next phase of my growth process (and yours) is called the *paidion* stage. The term *paidion* was used for children after they were approximately two years old, up to age eleven or twelve (before their bar-mitzvahs for Hebrew boys).[17]

During this stage, a person can learn obedience and service, but only if they do not rebel against it. The paidion believer can learn about deception and recognize true doctrine instead of false doctrine. If they do not learn this difference, they are susceptible to their imaginations running wild and following wild ideas. Paidions must be in good, solid fellowships to learn and grow in disciplined faith. What is most typical however, is that during this stage of life in the natural or physical world, a child begins to discover their own will and begins to want to do things in their own way. Rebellion can begin to show, and discipline is needed to correct it. In the spiritual realm, the same is true. Paidion believers seem to experience a resurgence of the Adamic nature and rebelliousness against the "rules" of Christian living. (Read more in Proverbs 13:24, 19:18, 22:15.)

I wanted to be all I needed to be in Jesus before I could approach the next season of my destiny. Like clay, I yielded myself *in the Maker's hands*. I gave Him access to my heart and my emotions. I took time to fast, study and pray. I kept busy attending church and spending as much time around other strong believers as possible. Yet, in this process, I made mistakes. I still dealt with some serious issues. I had to come to a place where my dependence had to come from my Father God alone and not from me. My Father wanted me to know Him dramatically in the power of His resurrection.

We may not understand the phase of our growth, yet the Father, in His omniscience, knows all. As we draw closer to Him, yielding to Him more and more, it becomes obvious that we will need Him in each season of our lives. We must allow the Father to mold us in His hand and deliver us from our inadequacies. As we surrender our soul-man to His process, God will expose every personal issue we have suppressed. His name is Jesus—the Heavenly Master Potter—our all-sufficient God.

Chapter 7

Preparing The Clay

How much more those who dwell in houses [bodies] of clay, whose foundations are in the dust. (Job 4:19 NIV)

Remember [earnestly], I beseech you, that you have fashioned me as clay [out of the same material, exquisitely and elaborately]. (Job 10:9 AMPC)

Behold, I am toward God and before Him even as you are; I also am formed out of clay [though I speak with abnormal wisdom because of divine illumination]. (Job 33:6 AMPC)

He drew me up out of a horrible pit [a pit of tumult and of destruction], out of the miry clay (froth and slime), and set my feet upon a

rock, steadying my steps and establishing my
goings. (Psalm 40:2 AMPC)

Before the potter can fire the clay, he must take it through
a preparation process. During this preparation stage, the potter must dry the raw clay, blend it back smooth with pure,
clean water to the right pliable consistency, then mold and
shape the clay on the wheel before it can be fired. All clay
must undergo this often-tedious preparation process; it is
deemed suitable if it does.

During this process, impurities found in the clay will be
exposed, dealt with, and removed. If these impurities are not
removed, it will cause the clay to discolor, warp, crack, and
even explode in the heat. Removing impurities at the beginning of the process helps the clay remain pliable and also to
retain its shape in the next drying and firing stages.

The Merriam-Webster dictionary defines clay as an
earthy material composed of fine particles of hydrous alu-
minum silicates and other minerals, and used for brick, tile,
and pottery.[18]

Prepared and conditioned clay is pliable and submits
to shaping and smoothing when moist, but it can be transi-
tioned by water or fire into other forms. Clay is hard when
fired or returns to *slip* when water is added before firing. Either way, this process is called a *transition stage*.

So it is with us. The human body is distinguished from the
Spirit as mud, dirt, or dust. For our potter's analogy, however,

we (the spirit being with a soul, not just an earthen body) are illustrated by the clay, and Jesus as our Master Potter.

> But now, O Lord, you are our Father; We are the clay, and You, our potter; And all we are the work of Your hand. (Isaiah 64:8 NKJV)

In this regard then, we must understand that clay is not greater than the Potter; we cannot walk, talk, think, or breathe without Him. Nevertheless, He chose us, His clay (not just the dirt or a mud vessel), to die for. As we glean from the revelation of our Father, the Potter, who holds the divine blueprint of the kind of vessel He desires, we realize the clay is in the care of his Maker's Hand.

The love of Jesus motivated Him to fashion us out of His own heart. The process began when we received Jesus as our Lord and personal Savior. In concurrence with clay, we experience the same transitional phases as clay. Remember, water is essential for the transitional phase of the development of the clay. Water symbolizes Jesus, the Word of God, and the Holy Spirit.

The metaphors of God's Word also include the idea of *cleansing power*. It is associated with water because water cleanses, prepares the clay:

> How can a young man cleanse his way? By taking heed according to your word. (Psalm 119:9 NKJV)

> You are already clean because of the word
> which I have spoken to you. (John 15:3 NKJV)

> That He might sanctify and cleanse it with
> the washing of water by the word. (Ephesians
> 5:26)

So, we see that the Potter is Jesus, and we are the clay. He does the shaping, molding, pounding, cleansing, and creating. Psalm 100:3 (NKJV) tells us that "it is He who has made us, not we ourselves."

He continues the creative process that began in Genesis. He is still working on us! The Potter, employing the work of the Holy Spirit, then, can be seen as the water. He uses the washing of the water of the Word to bring the clay to the right consistency, enabling Him to shape it, sanctify it, set it apart, and cleanse it. We are the church, and we are being cleansed with the washing of the water by the Word of Jesus.

Water is used as a type for the Holy Spirit of God. He will cleanse us in the spirit of our mind to bring about a divine transition from our original nature. The process is ongoing; therefore, Holy Spirit changes us from one degree to another, from one level to the next. Since the process occurs gradually, it may appear or look like nothing is happening on the outside; even though the process is slow, the Potter expects a permanent outcome by performing an inside endeavor.

When water is applied to clay, it increases plasticity and becomes more pliable. Plasticity refers to substances soft enough to be molded yet capable of hardening into the desired fixed form. Pliability suggests something can be easily bent, molded, or folded. In this state, the transformed clay is adaptive and can conform to whatever it is placed on. In our symbolic analogy of the clay, remember that we are the clay; at this stage, we must go through the transforming process, which may seem at times to be painful, unbearable, long, and grueling. Still, it is necessary for the desired outcome of our Lord.

In learning these things, the Holy Spirit ministered to me that we often resist being the clay in our Lord's hands because in our pridefulness, we do not understand the purpose or the will of our Father. So, we must humble ourselves. Humility is characterized by one yielding when you do not want to.

We can imagine that it requires much patience from the Father when dealing with strong-willed children (perhaps like dried out or hardened clay). And our loving Potter uses all the necessary tools in the Kingdom to get us there. The potter will use water, power, and fire while molding, forming, shaping, and finishing the project. We can view that perhaps as how our Lord God uses the power of the Holy Spirit, The Word of God, and refining Fire (life's crises) to increase our plasticity (so to speak), making us more pliable in our Father's hands. In our yielding to this work of His hands, He *will* lovingly take us from glory to glory. His Word tells us:

> Ye have not chosen me, but I have chosen
> you, and ordained you, that ye should go and

bring forth fruit, and that your fruit should remain: that whatsoever ye shall ask of the Father in my name, he may give it you. (John 15:16)

The God of our fathers hath chosen thee, that thou shouldest know his will, and see that Just One, and shouldest hear the voice of his mouth. (Acts 22:14)

But God hath chosen the foolish things of the world to confound the wise; and God hath chosen the weak things of the world to confound the things which are mighty. (1 Corinthians 1:27)

So we establish that the clay is not the Potter. The Potter is Jesus, our creator, originator, procreator, and fashioner. The clay cannot walk, talk, think, or breathe without the assistance of the Potter. However, God the Father chose us (the clay) from His heart to function and represent His Kingdom. The Potter knows the divine purpose for His clay (His children). The design choice for the vessel, the vessel's assignment, and the vessel's intended setting and useful purpose.

Just as our bodies have many parts and each part has a special function, so it is with Christ's body. We are many parts of one body, and we all belong to each other. (Romans 12:4–5 NLT)

... there are not only vessels of gold and of silver, but also of wood and of earth; and some to honour, and some to dishonour. If a man therefore purge himself from these, he shall be a vessel unto honour, sanctified, and meet for the master's use, and prepared unto every good work. (2 Timothy 2:20–23)

There are many kinds of vessels and varieties of clay (i.e., dry clay, pure white clay, and some comprised of other minerals and materials). For every vessel that the Potter envisions in His mind, He already knows what the clay will become *before he forms the vessel.* He also knows what it will take to make or fashion the vessel. The Father's wisdom processes every clay vessel with the divine intent for His purpose, not ours. It has been decided in the mind of the Potter beforehand.

Likewise, the clay does not yet know its destiny, purpose, potential, value, worth, identity, and abilities. We are the clay that the Father has chosen for His good pleasure. I am so glad He loved us enough to want to choose us for His kingdom to do His bidding! We are His vessel and we are in the Potter's hands, *in the Maker's hands.*

Our Creator has hand-picked us (chiseled and prepared) for a divine assignment formed according to His heartbeat, plans, blueprint, and design. We have been bought, redeemed, and purchased by the Blood of Jesus and are now placed in The Potter's House, The Kingdom of God, which is an exceptionally large place. We are now heirs and a part of His great Kingdom.

Isaiah 45:9 (NLT) says, "What sorrow awaits those who argue with their Creator. Does a clay pot argue with its maker? Does the clay dispute with the one who shapes it, saying, 'Stop, you are doing it wrong?' Does the pot exclaim, 'How clumsy can you be?'"

And Roman 9:20 (NLT) states, "No, don't say that. Who are you, a mere human being, to argue with God? Should the thing that was created say to the one who created it, 'Why have you made me like this?'"

Many of us (as the clay) constantly tell the Potter what He should be doing with our lives. It is common for humanity to think that because of education, accomplishments, titles, and positions in the Body of Christ, we can direct our own lives, tell others how to run their lives, and make our own decisions for our assignments and destinies. This is what is common to man, but the Bible has another viewpoint. It asks:

> How foolish can you be? He is the Potter, and he is certainly greater than you, the clay! Should the created thing say of the one who made it, "He didn't make me"? Does a jar ever say, "The potter who made me is stupid"? (Isaiah 29:16 NLT)

The nerve of us! When things do not go as we think, we quickly blame God. We discredit Him, become ungrateful and unthankful and tell God He missed the mark. We tell Him He does not understand what we are going through and that He has messed up. Humanity further tells our Father, "You have chosen the wrong person for this assignment. I do not possess the qualities or intellect to do this. I am unable to speak well; I am too dumb, too ugly, and I am too poor." When the worst comes to worst, we compare ourselves to clay vessels we deem to be in worse condition.

In rebellion, humanity regularly chooses to change the word of God by taking Scripture out of context to please and suit our purposes and desires. We have forgotten that He has chosen us; He has handpicked us, saved, delivered, cleansed, and sanctified us. Yet we have the boldness to demand our Father to change His agenda and plans while we act like we have the right to rebuke and reprove our God, the Potter. What are we doing at this point? We have jumped off the Potter's wheel and out of the Maker's hand. We have chosen to become the potter of our own clay. We have snatched the blueprint from His hand. Now we are holding the plans; we are giving the instructions. Instead of allowing Him to tell us the plans, we are trying to tell Him what to do, how to do it, when, where, and how it should be done.

Sometimes we act like we got it all together and are ready to instruct Him. We will say, "I know how to run my life! I got the plans, and I can take it from here." Does any of this sound familiar? All of this shows our immaturity in the Kingdom.

It is a typical picture of unconditioned clay, immature and impure in our behaviors or motivations.

At this stage, we must all experience our true transformation in our Father's intimate care—*in the Maker's hands.* Whenever we begin to rebel, resist, and complain while going through the process, we may have to ask ourselves, "Have I released all of my dross and residue to my God?"

God has chosen, handpicked, saved, delivered, and cleaned us up. The dealings of the Lord will expose all of the imperfections in our inner core. Our identity is still going through some challenges. I believe our heavenly Father, full of Grace, love, and mercy, looks at His foolish clay, shakes His head, and says, *"Wow!* I still have some work to do with this clay! I have just begun to do the work, and still, I am not finished with them. Like a fine honorable vessel, they must be *conditioned for use!"*

Chapter 8
Conditioning for Use

So far we have studied how the Master Potter has chiseled and prepared the raw materials. But before the vessel can be finished, unconditioned clay still needs the process called *conditioning*. And, like clay must be conditioned for use, so must we be developed for use.

We do not enter as adults when we are born again into the Kingdom of God. We come into the Kingdom just like we were birthed in the natural—as babes. I realize that I said this in a previous chapter, but it merits repeating. Paul, the apostle, wrote in 1 Corinthians 3:1 (ESV):

> But I, brothers, could not address you as spiritual people, but as people of the flesh, as infants in Christ.

In this verse, the Greek word for infants is nēpios, which we previously established means "an infant, little child... childish, untaught, unskilled."[19] Initially, like the natural, we behave as we do because of immaturity; we are underdeveloped spiritual sons and daughters. We must have spiritual parents to nurture, feed, and disciple us into our destiny according to God's purpose and plans.

So, we see that the Christian's life parallels our physical life in that we are born, then we must grow in wisdom and knowledge in Jesus. This process does not occur overnight. We are to attain maturity. Many never learn or have forgotten that once we are born into the Kingdom, there is a call always to be alive and live with the Lord. The Word of God teaches us the process in Romans 6:8–11 (NIV):

> Now if we died with Christ, we believe that we will also live with him. For we know that since Christ was raised from the dead, he cannot die again; death no longer has mastery over him. The death he died, he died to sin once for all; but the life he lives, he lives to God. In the same way, count yourselves dead to sin but alive to God in Christ Jesus.

> But grow in the grace and knowledge of our Lord and Savior, Jesus Christ. (2 Peter 3:18 NIV)

> Like newborn babies, you must crave pure spiritual milk so that you will grow into a full experience of salvation. (1 Peter 2:2 NLT)

And this is my prayer: that your love may abound more and more in knowledge and depth of insight. (Philippians 1:9 NIV)

Author Ron Graham expresses it this way:

When God by his grace, and by the virtue of Christ and his sacrifice, bestows his gift of forgiveness on those who obey him, then God has made them righteous. They should not say, "All our righteousness is like filthy rags" [Isaiah 64:4–9], but rather, "I am honored in the sight of the Lord, and God is my strength" [Isaiah 49:5].[20]

"When God by His Grace"… We must grow and mature by grace in the virtue of Christ Jesus. We must be made new experientially. We have been produced so that we also produce (re-produce, multiply). To *produce* is "to give birth or rise to yield,"[21] and to bring forth fruits representing the King we serve. We must yield and bring into existence the unseen supernatural abilities that originate in our Heavenly Father. He has already bestowed His gift of righteousness upon us, (those who have received Him as our Savior). However, we need further reproving, discipline, and equipping. We need to grow in the things of God, in the The Word of God.

To continue using our potter's terminology, we were considered contaminated, discarded, unconditioned clay, if you will, before entering the Kingdom of God. The word unconditioned denotes instinctive behavior and natural reflexes to which we are accustomed. We have not been taught or have not learned to follow the concepts of God's Word or His Kingdom. After we receive Jesus as our Lord and Savior, we are cleansed and redeemed by the blood of Jesus, no longer contaminated and discarded. In humility, we receive Him. He begins the renaturing process by taking away the contaminants. As we are transformed, we conclude our time as unconditioned clay, maturing in our destiny and His purpose and assignments.

What Is Unconditioned Clay?

> And now the Lord says—he who formed me in the womb to be his servant to bring Jacob back to him and gather Israel to himself, for I am honored in the eyes of the Lord, and my God has been my strength—he says:

> "It is too small a thing for you to be my servant to restore the tribes of Jacob and bring back those of Israel I have kept. I will also make you a light for the Gentiles, that my salvation may reach to the ends of the earth." (Isaiah 49:5–6 NIV)

Unconditioned clay still needs to be conditioned for use, shaped, smoothed, and, ultimately, put under fire. The "conditioning for use" stage must come to get us ready for the work or assignment Jesus desires us to fulfill in His Kingdom. In this stage, the believer's life is a process that will require humility, patience, obedience, submission, and willingness to believe in Jesus. Our responses during that preparation stage will determine the length of time we will stay in it.

We must have a mindset to be renewed in the Word of God daily. If we resist this process, our Potter is not at fault. We must be willing and choose to cooperate with the Potter while in the molding, drying, and firing process so we can be changed to the Master's design and plan for our lives.

> For He chose us in him before the creation of the world to be holy and blameless in his sight. In love, he predestined us for adoption to sonship through Jesus Christ, in accordance with his pleasure and will—to the praise of his glorious grace, which he has freely given us in the One he loves. (Ephesians 1:4–6 NIV)

Looking at the pottery-making process, I can understand again the wisdom of our Heavenly Father in choosing each of us to do what we have been assigned to do in His Kingdom. We are all uniquely made in our identity. Because of this uniqueness, our Heavenly Father knows what we can manage in the growth process. Therefore, we should never want to be a cheap imitation of someone else or rush the process at the expense of the result.

The Lord is completely aware of the assignment He wants us to serve; therefore, He knows what suits the clay (us). Jesus is a better judge than we are, and He has accurately chosen whom He wants to do certain things in His Kingdom. Ephesians 1:11–12 states,

> In him we were also chosen, having been predestined according to the plan of him who works out everything in conformity with the purpose of his will, in order that we, who were the first to put our hope in Christ, might be for the praise of his glory.

This is an impressive revelation because we have a Potter that loves us so much that He chose us on purpose. He hand-picked you and me to fulfill His will in the Kingdom. In this process, many find that they will either believe and continue in Christ or not believe and find excuses to give up while they are growing in the process.

Growing Through Sanctification

We established in chapter six that there is no accelerated mechanical process in the Kingdom of God. No, it will be completely different for the members of the Body of Christ. We are the finest quality vessels, made *in the Maker's hands*. The quality of a hand-made piece, made in the traditional way of the potter's wheel, reveals exquisite uniqueness and the most excellent quality.

We must allow the word of God to become alive inside of us. This will happen when we develop an intimate personal relationship with Jesus. We must have a prayer life; we grow in His faith so the renewing of our minds can transform us. We must spend time, even years or decades, with the Master Potter. This maturing, conditioning for use, is walking out our sanctification.

> I beseech you therefore, brethren, by the mercies of God, that ye present your bodies a living sacrifice, holy, acceptable unto God, which is your reasonable service. And be not conformed to this world: but *be ye transformed* by the renewing of your mind, that ye may prove what is that good, and acceptable, and perfect, will of God. (Romans 12:1–2)

Part of our transformation is in our *sanctification*. The Bible says that Christ Jesus *is* our sanctification.

> But of him are ye in Christ Jesus, who of God is made unto us wisdom, and righteousness, and sanctification, and redemption: That, according as it is written, He that glorieth, let him glory in the Lord. (1 Corinthians 1:30)

Knowing that—meaning knowing *Him*—we can better seek to understand, "*What* is sanctification?" According to Merriam Webster Dictionary, to sanctify is to "set apart to a sacred purpose or to religious use, to free from sin, to purify, to impart or impute sacredness, inviolability, or respect to, to give moral or social sanctions, to make productive of holiness or piety."[22]

So, Christ Jesus is our sanctification, and He works in us through the Holy Spirit to accomplish the work. He does not accomplish it through human flesh or the mindset of any leader or individual. We must take our time with Jesus while we are in this process. Sanctification is not something we put on, pull off, dress up, or strip away.

We cannot cry, have a pity party, manipulate, seduce, or try to sway the Holy Spirit in any way to move on our part before He is ready. We must learn our identity in the Kingdom in this process. It takes time to renew our minds. The more we choose to renew our minds, we will establish our identity, which is in Christ Jesus Our Lord. We must understand Whom we possess inside of us, believing with all our heart, mind, and soul that we are (have been made) the righteousness of God in Jesus Christ.

Holy Spirit has you in mind. He has the blueprint and specifications for your destiny. At this stage and process, He knows how long it will take for you to be strengthened in the inner man and to endure what is coming next. Therefore, we must be patient and not grow weary in well doing (Galatians 6:9). If we do not yield to the process, the desired outcome may be delayed in our lives. Holy Spirit wants us to be soluble, submerged, and completely engulfed in His presence. This will allow the spirit of our mind, our soulish man, to yield as we should before moving into the next stage of development.

Chapter 9

Shaping and Smoothing

Before the Father can fire the clay, it must be shaped and smoothed. There are many of you going through things right now (life's circumstances) that seem to be bending you all out of shape. However, if you endure this process, the Father will help you understand it. We all must be able to take the shaping of the Lord. The smoothing process is another step Jesus used to mature us in our destiny, which is to become fully mature. So, what is this *shaping and smoothing process?*

Jeremiah 1:5 (NLT) states,

> I knew you before I formed you in your mother's womb. Before you were born I set you apart and appointed you as my prophet to the nations.

God knew us before we were conceived in our mothers' wombs. Before your father knew your mother, God had you in His heart and mind. Jesus knew our destiny before we were introduced to our parents' bodies. The phrase *set apart* means to be consecrated, sanctified, or blessed for a specific purpose or assignment. Jeremiah was declared by God a prophet before he was born. He was a seer set in the office as a Prophet of God before the Nations. Likewise, with us, we have a God who is an intentional Father.

Someone may ask, what does shaping and smoothing have to do with the Father preparing us for our destiny? In the previous chapters, we have seen how we are the clay in God's hand. We grow through seasons of maturity as we develop in our lives in the Kingdom. The process of becoming fully mature is a lifelong process. The chiseling, preparing, conditioning, shaping and smoothing all allow us to be fit for the proper assignment.

> O Lord, give me understanding according to thy word. Let my supplication come before thee: Deliver me according to thy word. (Psalm 119:169–170)

Yielding to this shaping and smoothing process of equipping will help us and require us to know Jesus. We must understand Him from the word of God. Our untrained and undisciplined minds must go through a transformation.

Roman 12:2 tells us "not to be conformed to this world but be ye transformed by the renewing of your mind, that ye may prove what is that good and acceptable, and perfect, will of God." So, there is this great battle that rages for mastery over the mind of mankind.

From the beginning of time, Jesus deliberately hand-picked us (chiseled, shaped, and smoothed) to fulfill an assignment in His Kingdom. However, mankind has struggled with surrendering his total will and life over to the hands of His Maker. Man has been searching for who he is since the fall of Adam. This disconnect has caused us to make foolish choices in search of our identity.

He has the blueprint for our DNA. An acronym for DNA is Divine Non-negotiable Atom. An *atom* is the smallest essential unit of ordinary matter that constitutes a living element. Every solid, liquid, gas, and plasma are composed of neutral or ionized atoms. Atoms are extremely small. The term *atom* comes from the Greek word for *indivisible* because it was once thought that atoms were the smallest things in the universe and could not be divided.[23]

Looking at an atom and the word of God as an analogy; an atom may be small in nature; however, it is essential for every living thing on this planet. The Word of God is the expressed energy, life, light, and thoughts manifested from the Father. We should never view it as insignificant, small, or worthless.

God in His Omniscience chose to make mankind. He chose us unlike any other creatures or beings. It was marvelous He decided to create us. We were made after His image. The uniqueness of the creation of mankind, a speaking, thinking, creative being, having the intelligence to choose and decide like God, and to be able to communicate with God and as God for what he wants.

Genesis 1:27 (NIV) says, "So God created mankind in his own image, in the image of God he created them; Male and female he created them." And, further Genesis 2:7 states, "Then the Lord God formed a man from the dust of the ground and breathed into his nostrils the breath of life, and the man became a living being."

Our destiny was in the heart and the mind of God. When God created us, He never sees us as unimportant in any way. His purpose was and is to have a speaking being He would be able to commune and have fellowship with.

Nevertheless, we may see ourselves unimpressive in the presence of our Maker. The Lord is still asking mankind today the same question that he asked Israel centuries ago:

> This is the word that came to Jeremiah from the LORD: "Go down to the potter's house, and there I will give you, my message." So I went down to the potter's house, and I saw him working at the wheel. But the pot he was shaping from the clay was marred in his hands; so, the potter formed it into another pot, shaping it as it seemed best to him. Then the word of the LORD came to me. He said, ***"Can I not do with you, Israel, as this potter does?"*** declares the LORD. "Like clay in the hand of the potter, so are you in my hand..." (Jeremiah 18:1–6 NIV; emphasis added)

We live in a day and time in which this scripture text is vitally important. God deliberately seeks us. He often chooses busy people. Many times we do not expect that an Omnipotent God would consider us for anything in His kingdom. But He does!

The Father takes our lives and **shapes** them according to His blueprint. He has ordained and predetermined our courses. He works diligently with us because our lives are unfiltered and marred in so many cases. We are messed up before coming into Christ. However, we have a loving, gracious Father that created us from the dust of the earth and has invested Himself in us.

Jesus is our model for surrendering to the perfect will of God. Sometimes we think we know what is best for ourselves, our families, our ministries, and careers. Consequently, we fail to allow Jesus to be the Potter—shaper and smoother—the Lord of our lives. As believers we are required to have a constant renewing of the image, or pattern from the Word in our minds. Mind renewal will create a glow of divine essence or quality of our Lord Jesus that radiates from within us.

The shaping and smoothing process is just another element the Father uses to develop us in creating a love union with Christ.

The Lord can *use* indirect strategies such as families, our marriages, our finances, children, our jobs, sicknesses, or diseases to recapture our focus. (God does not put any of these negative things on His children. He is our protector. But He will turn them for our good and teach us things as we walk through them.) We must be confident and know that this process assists us in our growth.

The thought pattern of the Lord must become our pattern of thinking. We must choose to allow God's Word to transform our thoughts; we must agree with His thoughts and ways. This will ultimately bring about total transformation in our lives as we recognize and obey God's directions. God's Word is our source for inspiration and revelation to discern His perfect will.

We also must discern with a proper attitude when the enemy comes to attack us. We must call unto the Lord (Jeremiah 33:3). He will never let us be in a situation where He will not be with us. We must ask God to help us in every situation. He is our Shepherd (Psalm 23:1–6). We will go through our struggles in life, but the Lord—our Master Potter—is with us, always seeking to bring us to the fullness of purpose. He uses angelic visitations, the Rhema (spoken, revealed) Word of God, the Lord's written Word, the Logos, and prophetic declarations. It may not always make sense to us; however, we must be in tune with Holy Spirit. He is our Potter, and we are His clay. God will give us aide and strategies, but we must know Him so that we know our instruction is from the Lord.

The whole process may seem brutal to our emotions and soulish man, but we cannot afford to distrust the voice of the Lord. When the soul man is under construction, many times it will resist this transformation. This is why we must renew our minds daily in the Word of God. God has placed leaders, instructors, mentors, and teachers in the body to position us with favor that will cause us to mature. Christ's compassion in them will allow these people to go out of their way to help us when we become submissive individuals *in the Maker's hands.*

This is important because postponement or procrastination is disobedience. We must resolve that once we hear, we must also decide to respond. We cannot respond like the rich young ruler. We cannot react despondently like blind Bartimaeus. We aren't waiting for someone else to put us in the water, or waiting for an angel to stir it in order to receive a blessing from God. (You can explore this more in Matthew 19:16–29 and Matthew 5:4–7.)

Keep in mind that our dependency is on Jesus, our Master Potter, and not on others. It is imperative that we lay aside all fears and refuse to get offended. There is this propensity to believe we can do or be who we are on our own without the Master's help. Nevertheless, when we humble ourselves and realize we are nothing without Him, we will find our breakthrough in His Kingdom. We must move with quick obedience in that moment when we believe, perceive, and understand the Lord's voice. The urgency of obedience and humility is predicated on the choice we make for the Kingdom of God. Not only will it bless our lives, but it will affect the lives of others. This kind of obedience and unselfishness results from our own shaping but can save the lives of many.

Once chiseled, prepared, conditioned, then shaped and smoothed, the clay is still considered *green.* The potter calls this *greenware,* and is mindful of that state. Even clay that might appear to be dried out (aged)—if it has not been put in the fire, that clay is considered *green*.

Our Master Potter knows even more perfectly that we are still green. In our development, just like the clay, being green is a state of immaturity and inexperience. Being green will cause us to be self-righteous and selfish. It may show up in the form of arrogance and pride. It may cause us to think we know it all. Therefore, the refining process must come to bring development to our lives.

So we see, even in forming the vessel, that patience is a virtue that must be cultivated in all of us. Our Master Potter will never hurry to get us to our intended purpose. Therefore, we must allow the fruit of patience to have its perfect work.

Chapter 10
The Firing Process

Once the clay has been prepared, conditioned, shaped and smoothed (or molded by hand on the potter's wheel) into an earthen vessel of greenware, it can move to the final stages of development... the firing process!

On a visit to *The Pottery Wheel*, I discovered that the three most common types of finished clay pottery "are earthenware, stoneware, and porcelain. Stoneware clay and porcelain are capable of becoming harder and denser than earthenware. Earthenware clay is a 'low fire clay' that usually becomes as hard as possible during the second stage firing or the bisque fire. By contrast, stoneware and porcelain will continue to harden [and become more dense] in later firings. Stoneware and porcelain are known as 'mid or high-fire clays,' which mature at higher temperatures than a bisque firing. So, earthenware is mature after a bisque fire. Stoneware and porcelain are semi-mature and still have a way to go before they mature."[24]

What can we take away from that discovery? Like the differences in types of clay above, we must understand that many of us can endure more than others because Father God knows who will mature at a different time and on a different level than others. What you require is already in the knowledge of the Master Potter and it is written in the specification of your destiny and your assignment.

There are three stages to the firing process: drying, bisque firing, and the glazing fire. Let's walk through each of these phases and how that applies to our own maturing process with God.

Bone Dry Vessels

In the first stage of the firing process, the green clay, or greenware, must be dried out thoroughly. To quote one professional potter, "The best way to dry your pottery is slowly and naturally. This allows your clay to dry naturally without trying to speed up the process."[25]

When the greenware is completely dry, it is called ***bone-dry clay***. Clay must be allowed to reach this stage before you actually fire it. Inside the kiln, the special oven-like furnace for firing pottery and ceramics, any remaining moisture will eventually reach the boiling point of water at 212F (100C) and become steam. When water turns to steam, it expands. Suppose, despite preparing the clay with care, some tiny air pockets are left in your pottery when that moisture in the clay turns into steam. In that case, the steam will expand quickly into any air pockets and cause your piece to explode![26]

How does this apply to our transformation process? We may already see things taking shape in this drying-out stage of our development. For example, we may sense that the Lord wants us to go and start a ministry. However, we are still full of moisture (hot air and steam) at this phase of being called or chosen. We become self-absorbed in what we think rather than knowing what the Father wants from us. Or we may find that our Potter does not choose us to do the kind of ministry we thought we were operating in. Some might say that we are still inexperienced at this point. Our clay has yet to dry out before it is ready for firing.

What does this look like in a real world application? When difficulties and problems begin to hit, we explode, often along with everything around us. Remember, it is never the Lord's intention for any of us to explode! But, if that is what it takes for us to be humble and pliable in our Potter's hand, let the explosion begin!

As God's children, we become self-deceived if we do not humble ourselves to submit to our Lord's discipline. Satan uses people to whisper in our ears to swell our egos (like moisture in the clay). Out of ignorance, we get puffed up in ambition (like the air pockets in pottery that are full of stream). We refuse to listen to sound instructions from our leaders and mentors.

One of the saddest outcomes for members of the body of Christ is to refuse to humble ourselves and admit that we are in error and have missed it. Our development is a slow, slow process. It does not happen overnight. The process may be painful at its outset, much like the long-processed bone-dry clay. But Romans 12:7–8 gives us great help, saying:

Let us wait on our ministering: or he that teaches, on teaching; or he that exhorted, on exhortation: he that giveth, let him do it with simplicity; he that ruled, with diligence; he that sheweth mercy, with cheerfulness.

We can take inventory of our lives right now. Are you experiencing dryness or perpetuating circumstances that seem never to end? Perhaps you feel your season has lasted too long? You may think life is unfair or God has forsaken you. You might feel... bone dry, fragile, and even broken. "Bone dry pottery, that has not been fired, is still raw clay. Bone dry clay is:

Fragile – it breaks very easily. If it gets gently knocked by accident, it will shatter and details like handles will break off easily.

Soluble – if you submerge bone dry clay in water it will dissolve and return to its plastic workable state."[27]

Bone-dry clay is not really practical nor useful. So why would God often want us to remain at length in this bone-dry stage? Because greenware that is now bone-dry, molded clay is still *soluble*. Our Father God wants us first to be soluble. Why is remaining for a season in a soluble stage important? Submerging bone-dry clay in water will dissolve and return to its pliable, shapeable state. This is the value of solubility!

This reminds me of these scripture passages:

> The vessel that he made of clay was marred in the hand of the potter; so, he made it again into another vessel, as it seemed good to the potter to make. (Jeremiah 18:4)

> But in a great house there are not only vessels of gold and silver, but also of wood and clay, some for honor and some for dishonor. Therefore, if anyone cleanses himself from the latter, he will be a vessel for honor, sanctified and useful for the Master, prepared for every good work. (2 Timothy 2:20–21 NKJV)

The Lord knows what it will take to remain soluble so that He may form us into "a vessel of honor, sanctified and useful for the Master, prepared for every good work" (v. 21). The reward will be very fruitful when we yield and submit to our Master Potter's perfect process.

Into The Fire (The Bisque Firing)

In the analogy of a potter and clay, Holy Spirit is the Spirit of the Master Potter. As we yield to Him, He can turn the fire(s) of affliction for our good to expose and burn out impurities in our lives. Under His expert care, the fire of affliction will purify, burn off, and sanctify us. It is our refining. It is part of the process.

> Behold, I have refined thee, but not with silver; I have chosen thee in the furnace of affliction. (Isaiah 48:10)

The fire of affliction may present as a disappointment, the loss of a child, sickness, disease, or any other circumstance. The key thing to remember is that our Father God, The Master Potter, will not put any of these things on His children. No one relishes pain, suffering, and struggles; however, these things will come in life. Only *in the Maker's hands* can we see the fiery trials be turned for our benefit and be used to grow us into maturity.

God wants all of us to be strengthened by fire—not fragile and easily duped by our adversary, satan. That finishing work comes through the firing process. After the pottery is bone dry, it will be fired twice. The first time is called the bisque fire (or biscuit firing). During the first firing, clay is transformed from greenware to ceramic material.

Our previous text taught us that greenware is fragile, breaks easily, and is soluble (if it gets wet, it will dissolve). Progressing in the process, the *bisque-ware* produced by a bisque fire is hardened but still porous. If bisque-ware gets wet, it will absorb water *but does not dissolve*. Once the clay has gone through the change from greenware to bisque-ware, it cannot return to its previous state.[28] ***Think about that!***

During this bisque firing phase, the clay was put into the hottest fire thus far. In our case, the Master Potter puts His clay in the kiln because He knows the vessel's purpose. Its assignment has already been predestined in the mind of the Potter. *The firing is required for the vessel's readiness for its intended use.* And it ensures we do not return to the previous state of impurity or fragility.

Like the clay pot, we suffer heated circumstances and question what is going on in our lives. At this point, we must trust Jesus and know Jesus has our lives in His hands. The firing process may feel like growing pains. The soul of man must learn true submission while experiencing trauma, discomfort, and disappointments.

It is so fitting to our discussion that it is during this bisque firing that the clay begins to mature. Yes, that is right. Clay is said to be mature when bonded together, as dense and hard as possible. It is also interesting that some types of clay can become much denser and harder than others.

We may not understand the process during our unique developmental stages, but we must learn to endure each season with hope. The Father will not allow you to go through more than you can manage. James 1:12–13 (NIV) says:

> Blessed is the one who perseveres under trial because, having stood the test, that person will receive the crown of life that the Lord has promised to those who love him. When tempted, no one should say, "God is tempting

me." For God cannot be tempted by evil, nor
does he tempt anyone.

The glory we house inside us is the Holy Spirit himself. We received this great anointing in the new birth experience. But we must all go through the development process as we grow in grace. Holy Spirit will snatch back the curtains of our destiny to reveal or give us a glimpse into our destiny to encourage us, so let us not grow weary or impatient. The purpose of the Father is intentional. Therefore, He will allow us to go through what we are going through to fulfill His plans. It is at this point that He is still working on us. We must not allow our emotions to get in the way. At this stage, we must not compare our tests to someone else.

And with the clay? Now we see a vessel arriving at a mature stage, less likely to break when handled and fewer impurities remaining. What is next? While there are many kilns (fires of affliction), the stages of firing clay remain the same. We are ready for the final change, the last stage of firing.

The Blazing Fire

As I researched this firing process, I also learned from *The Pottery Wheel* that several layers of glaze are often applied to a piece of bisque-ware before firing. The number of layers varies depending on the method of application and the glaze used. The potter must choose a glaze suitable for the clay in hand. Once the glaze is applied and has dried, the vessel is ready for its second firing. During the *glaze fire*, the ingredients in the glaze transform. In a glaze fire, the clay itself continues to mature. Like clay, the glaze also matures.[29]

Please consider that the Heavenly Father begins the whole process by chiseling our raw material, preparing and conditioning the unconditioned clay, shaping and smoothing us for greater works. Why? Jesus knows the process is to help us achieve our destiny and purpose in His Kingdom. Jesus cannot and will not display unconditioned, wet, immature clay to represent Him. Maturing us is His divine strategy and purpose for His children.

The blazing fire matures the vessel for the intended use. *The finished work matures in the fire.*

Chapter 11
Hidden Treasure Within

In the history recorded in 1 Chronicles 22:2, we see that King David ordered the resident foreigners in the land to be called together. He appointed some of them stonecutters to chisel stones for the building of God's temple. Chosen by King David, they were a generation drafted out of darkness and planted in the Kingdom of our Lord.

In fulfillment of that prophetic type and shadow, Jesus saw the value and worth of generations of people drafted out of darkness and planted in the Kingdom of our Lord. We learn in Hebrews 12:2 that Jesus, "… who for the joy that was set before him endured the cross, despising the shame, and is set down at the right hand of the throne of God."

He endured for the joy (us) that was set before him. We were adopted into the family of royalty. We have been called to dwell together in a land He has established. We are no longer considered foreigners, immigrants, or aliens without a home. We were once strangers, but now we are gathered unto the Lord. We are chosen ones, supernaturally anointed as skilled craftsmen in the Kingdom of God.

Like the craftsmen that David appointed, the Lord chose the Five-Fold members of the body of Christ to be handy craftsman that would build the temple of the Lord, the Church. As we look at the purpose, the heart, and the intention of God, these handy craftsmen were not only the chosen Israelites, but they were Gentiles that He saw into the future. They would be instrumental in helping to build the temple, the Body of Christ activated in Kingdom ministry.

While we were yet strangers, Jesus, in all His plans, chiseled, prepared, conditioned, shaped and smoothed us that we might be a part of this glorious work in His Kingdom. Strangers were the masons—hewers of stones to build the house of God. Your true value is being born for the glory of His Kingdom. Unfortunately, many have not yet understood our true worth and identity. He chose us.

> Ye also, as lively stones, are built up a spiritual house, an holy priesthood, to offer up spiritual sacrifices, acceptable to God by Jesus Christ.
>
> But ye are a chosen generation, a royal priesthood, an holy nation, a peculiar people; that ye should shew forth the praises of him who hath called you out of darkness into his marvellous light. (1 Peter 2:5, 9)

It was at this point in my own process that I came to know Him intimately. We all must come to grips with this in our lives. We must know Jesus as Savior; we must also know that we are His ambassadors or representatives of His Kingdom on this planet. We must believe that we are of excellent value in the sight of our God.

Do you know who lives in you? Do you know the power you possess within? Do you know that there is a treasure locked up inside of you just waiting to be unveiled? If we desire to truly know the answer to these questions, we must look to our Father God, who is our Abba, our Daddy. How wonderful! Just think about it! All born again believers are connected to the Creator of the universe. Oh! How special that makes you and me! The greatest anomaly we have is that we do not understand who we are, what we have, and how important we are to our Father.

The hidden treasure within will never be realized or understood if we fail to get acquainted with the one who initiated everything.

> But we have this treasure in jars of clay to show that this all-surpassing power is from God and not from us. (2 Corinthians 4:7 NIV)

We must realize everything that was created by our Father is going through the process of maturing. The Grace of Jesus is given to us to believe and receive the plans of God for our destiny.

> They said to him, "Inquire of God, please,
> that we may know whether our way on which
> we are going will be prosperous." The priest
> said to them, "Go in peace; your way in which
> you are going has the Lord's approval." (Judg-
> es 18:5–6 NASB)

In essence, we must inquire of the Lord what it is that we need to know that concerns us. We must not take anything for granted. God cares about everything in our lives. So, go ahead and ask him. It does not matter where you are or what you are going through in this season of your life. We must be hungry and passionate enough to seek Him about our lives and where we are going.

There came a time when, although I knew I was born again, I wanted to know how God saw me. I was desperate, hungry, and dissatisfied with my growth. So, I finally prayed to the Lord and said, *"Father, how do you see me?"*

Jesus was about to bring me to a greater understanding of my self-worth. He would show me what He found worthy or considered valuable to others. Jesus already knew my real worth and how He would use it to glorify His name. *The revelation I needed was to understand and believe that God has a profound love for me.* As my heavenly Father, He saw me as extremely valuable. My worth and value to Him motivated His love for me. We all are valuable to Jesus. Yet, we may find it difficult to understand. The apostle Paul wrote of this great longing, his desire for the Ephesians (and for us)...

That you may really come to know practically, through experience for yourselves, the love of Christ, which far surpasses mere knowledge without experience; that you may be filled through all your being unto all the fullness of God, may have the richest measure of the divine Presence, and become a body wholly filled and flooded with God Himself. (Ephesians 3:19 AMPC)

Lively Stones

Although we have used the analogy of the Master Potter all throughout this book, it is in this chapter that God chose to speak to us about the Hidden Treasure Within. Earlier in this chapter, we said,

> "while we were yet strangers, Jesus, in all His plans, chiseled, prepared, conditioned, shaped, and smoothed us that we might be a part of this glorious work in His Kingdom. Strangers were the masons—hewers of stones to build the house of God. Your true value is being born for the glory of His Kingdom."

In yet another pictorial analogy, God shows us that we are those stones! And together, we are being built up into a spiritual house. When I had finally prayed to the Lord and said, *"Father, how do you see me?"* The Lord said to me, *"You are my diamond."* This word to my heart fit perfectly with His Word and I finally saw it!

I saw that we are beautiful precious gems. Some may be rubies, diamonds, sapphires, turquoise, amethyst, emeralds, beryls, and more. Nevertheless, we are all of excellent value in the sight of our God. (Supporting this is the prophetic type and shadow of the stones on the priestly garments, which represented the twelve tribes who were God's people at that time—they pointed to us! Living stones.)

As I grew and matured in the things of God, the Lord continued to draw my attention to the process and the stages diamonds must go through to display such quality, timeless beauty, and durability. From there, I knew I had to study more about diamonds.

I still pondered the thought in my mind: God said I was His diamond! He loves me enough to say, "You are my diamond." This is a weighty statement. It left me toiling to believe, understand, and identify as a diamond. Think about this: A diamond is a priceless jewel hidden from the public until it is ready to be displayed! While that is a metaphor for us as we are developed by God, The Smithsonian Institute tells us this metaphor is accurate:

> Diamonds are formed deep within the Earth about 100 miles or so below the surface in the upper mantle. Obviously in that part of the Earth it's very hot. There's a lot of pressure, the

weight of the overlying rock bearing down, so that combination of high temperature and high pressure is what's necessary to grow diamond crystals in the Earth. As far as we know, all diamonds that formed in the Earth formed under those kinds of conditions…

The diamonds that we see at the surface are ones then that are brought to the surface by a very deep-seated volcanic eruption. It's a very special kind of eruption, thought to be quite violent, that occurred a long time ago in the Earth's history. We haven't seen such eruptions in recent times. They were probably at a time when the earth was hotter, and that's probably why those eruptions were more deeply rooted. These eruptions then carried the already-formed diamonds from the upper mantle to the surface of the Earth. When the eruption reached the surface it built up a mound of volcanic material that eventually cooled, and the diamonds are contained within that. These are the so-called Kimberlites that are typically the sources of many of the world's mined diamonds.

One of the things we know, therefore, about any diamonds that were brought to the surface is that the process of the Kimberlite erup-tion bringing the diamonds from the upper mantle to the surface of the Earth had to hap-pen very quickly, because if they were travel-ing too long and too slowly they would have literally turned into graphite along the way. And so by moving quickly they essentially got locked into place into the diamond structure. Once the diamonds have been brought from high temperature to low temperature very quickly—and by quickly, we mean in a matter of hours—these eruptions, these Kimberlite pipes moving to the surface, may have been traveling at rates of 20 to 30 miles per hour. Once the diamonds are brought to the surface and cooled relatively quickly, those carbon at-oms are locked into place and there's just not enough energy to now start rearranging them into graphite.[30]

Even as I discovered these facts about the diamond, I still struggled to understand this revelation of who I am and how Jesus sees me. Because of immaturity, it was necessary to re-main as hidden treasure, to grow through seasons of pressure and being processed—to stay hidden *in the Maker's hands.* As I continued with the Lord and the study of diamonds, I also learned that this is true at all phases of life, especially when the Lord has great work for us to fulfill. We must understand and trust that our times and seasons are in His hands.

I began to experience Holy Spirit-filled dreams and visions. He showed me all type of colors that were vibrant—yet beyond the eye's beauty. The revelations of these dreams and visions were unapparent to me. Therefore, I became troubled and inquired of the Lord about their meaning. My first reference point was the Word of God.

While I was seeking the Lord, Holy Spirit led me to study the priestly ministry. *There were the gemstones!* I also studied the major and minor prophets. These studies went on for some time. Yes, I believe they also related to the process of the *hidden treasure within* me being revealed! I hope you are beginning to see that **not only has the Master Potter created an exquisite, honorable vessel, He has place glorious hidden treasure within each vessel!**

While attending Sunday school, Bible study, and prayer services, I was able to comprehend and gain some revelations and impartation. My pastor assisted me in my studies. However, I still had many unanswered questions.

The ministry I associated with did not have a discipleship class for newborn believers. After receiving Jesus as Lord and Savior, we were instructed to attend church, pay our tithes, and find something to do in the church. As an educator, I had no problem submitting to authority. I began serving in the work of the ministry. I taught Sunday School, worked with the children's ministry, became a choir member, led a prayer band in a different area of my community, and assisted the minister of music in our church. Since I was single, I kept busy to stay focused on the things of God.

What I did not yet realize was that *our spiritual development doesn't depend on all the things we can be involved in!* Jesus patterned training people to become disciples **before** He commissioned them as apostles. All newborn believers need to be parented by the five-fold ministry gifts. (You can read more on these in Ephesian 4:8–11.) The church often can unwittingly produce spiritual renegades when equipping, instruction, and training are inadequate. And so it was for me that the youth in the ministry experienced some unbelievable difficulty.

We were left to figure out many spiritual things on our own. Many things came from other minister leaders, friends, trial by error, and even the enemy. The correction we received came from the pulpit when the Pastor preached on Sunday morning or during Bible study. Personal correction was administered by lay ministers instead of the overseer. The laity often resisted the correction. This was equivalent to untrained teenagers left with lay leadership attempting to discipline babies. This resulted in spiritual renegades trying to do ministry. Unfortunately at the time, I was one of those renegades.

Every son and daughter of the Kingdom must understand that we are gifted of our Father to work in His Kingdom. The revelation of this truth was not made known in my heart. This was not shared with us because we had not been trained effectively in leadership. The only ministry we knew about in the church was the ministry of teaching, pulpit preaching, missionary, pastoring, and evangelizing.

When the Holy Spirit began to impress upon my heart that He had a calling on my life for ministry, I struggled with it. So, I kept it to myself. My greatest joy was intercessory prayer. I loved spending time with Jesus. I could not wait to run into His throne room and lay prostrate in his presence. It was my favorite pastime and brought me great fulfillment. I did not realize it, but through the time spent in intercessory prayer, I was being transformed (metamorphóō) slowly in the presence and the Glory of God! When we spend time in the presence of the Lord, true transformation shapes our lives from within, and we emerge with a new mindset.

In the Greek, metamorphóō [Strong's #G3339] is (from 3326 /metá, "change after being with" and 3445 /morphóō, "changing form in keeping with inner reality") – properly, transformed after being with; transfigured. That Greek word is the root of the English terms "metamorphosis" and "meta-morphize" [*metamorphose.*][31] Merriam-Webster dictionary tells us that *metamorphose* is a transitive verb meaning: to change into a different physical form especially by supernatural means; to change strikingly the appearance or character of: TRANSFORM.[32]

The more I studied the word of God the more I could hear Jesus speak to my heart about myself and other people. I was having open visions of spiritual things that no one else could see or had experienced. When I shared my experiences with others, I realized the Lord was using some of the other women in our prayer circle in special ways as well. However, I felt the way He was using me was different and I dared not try to explain it because it appeared to them as being competitive.

My experiences were real. Those in the midst of me had been saved longer than me. I questioned why my Father was revealing Himself to me in these ways. I thought maybe it was this renegade spirit that was rising up inside of me with pride. We were not trained in the gifts of the Spirit, and I did not yet understand Body ministry or how to operate successfully in God's Kingdom.

I did not understand that the treasure embedded in me was not ready to be displayed. However, I moved in confidence. I was unashamed and fearless as the Holy Spirit revealed to me what He wanted me to do. These lessons in discernment and humility were part of my transformation.

I continued serving in the ministry at my Church. I was four years old in the Kingdom. When the Lord filled me with His Holy Spirit, it felt as if all hell came against me. I knew the Lord was calling me for greater works in His Kingdom for ministry, but I still would not yield. Temptation and persecution came from family, from my job, and the desire for companionship was being fanned before me. Some of these things came to captivate and draw me away from my commitment to serve in the Kingdom with Jesus. I seem to be erupting.

Little did I know Jesus was causing these eruptions and impurities to surface! Like a diamond, I was being sent through the heat to the surface! Like greenware, I was being refined and conditioned! Do you remember what happens to the clay pot with impurities and air bubbles? It explodes. Why were these lessons necessary? Because He was purifying and transforming the precious treasure within me. The word of the Lord says:

> All Scripture is breathed out by God and profitable for teaching, for reproof, for correction, and for training in righteousness, that the man of God may be complete, equipped for every good work. (2 Timothy 3:16–17 ESV)

I was vulnerable to distractions and temptations because of intimidation, but also because of a lack of training and equipping for the work of the ministry.

> The Lord said, "My people are destroyed for the lack of knowledge; because you have rejected knowledge, I reject you from being a priest to me. And since you have forgotten the law of your God, I also will forget your children." (Hosea 4:6 ESV)

We must identify where we are in our relationship with the Lord in complete honesty. This will enable us to come into full alignment with him. When the fullness of time for God has come, we must render unto Him an eternal "*Yes*."

The night before one Easter Sunday I had a divine visitation from an angel. The description of this angel was unlike anyone I had ever seen. He was wearing the most beautiful vibrant sapphire blue robe out of this world. His hair was dark black in color, and his face glowed. He told me not to be afraid. He was there to give me a message. I was given instructions to go. He said "I am appointing and penning this badge on you. It read, "*Deliverance*." He showed me the badge closer, and I looked at it. It also said, "Everyone that receives the Word I give you, they will be delivered, and those who rejected it will not be delivered."

In this visitation, I was immediately taken from my bedroom and was traveling up and down the community sharing the Word of God. Eventually, I found myself back in my room sitting up on my bed. I was instructed to go and share His Word. *Until the Word could become Rhema to me, I struggled to receive God's truth about my worth and value.* After that encounter, I had no problem going to my pastor to let him know what the Lord told me to do. I was confident that He sent me with an anointing to share the Word of the Lord.

If you are as challenged with your self-worth as I was, God wants you to know and see your true worth in His Kingdom. Like many others over the centuries, I was faced with believing in His great love and walking by faith or dismissing it. Whatever our issues, we all are faced with believing or not believing the Word of God daily. However, when we grow in the knowledge of God's love, which the Father has freely rendered, we find everything we need to be accepted in His Beloved. *We must believe that it is so.*

The Father had prepared me to experience some seasons of finishing. I thank God that in my journey of overcoming and maturing, I was not going to experience these episodes of development alone.

We must trust the Father with confident expectation, knowing that He loves us unconditionally. It is not how much we love Him that counts, but how much He loves us. It is important to settle how we view ourselves. *Will we agree with God?* The attributes and characteristics of the Father's Kingdom abides within all of us during spiritual conception. All we have to do is believe.

Everything we need has been deposited within us to fulfill our assignment. We were predestined from the foundation of the world to be His representative. Our destiny was established in Him before we were born. As born-again believers in Christ, there is a rich treasury—hidden treasure within—that has been deposited in everyone us, given to us by our Father. We must begin to believe with unwavering faith that our destiny was secure in the heart of God as a finished work, a settled matter, before our father knew our mother. We have been chiseled, prepared, conditioned, shaped and smoothed and fired as a new creation *in the Maker's hands.* It is now for us to discover all the glorious treasure that He has placed within us, His newly created vessel!

Chapter 12

Destined Before Birth

> We have obtained an inheritance, having been predestined according to His purpose who works all things after the counsel of His will. (Ephesians 1:11 NASB)

What is destiny and what does it have to with birth? Destiny is your expected end; it is your purposed destination. And this *destination* is divinely connected to your *origination*. You see, we were born to earthy parents in this world. We appeared with no instructions. Our parents did not possess a manual or a guide to help them to raise us. Some of us came here unwanted and unplanned. Others were planned and welcomed and ready to be received.

Regardless of the natural circumstance, the Word of God assures us that we (you) are here because our Father God wanted us (you) to show up in this world to share in His Kingdom family. Merriam Webster dictionary defines *destiny* as "a predetermined course of events often held to be an irresistible power or agency." It also implies something foreor-dained and suggests a great noble course or end.[33] The scripture above in Ephesians says we were predestined according to **His purpose.** That is true destiny. Before the foundation of the world, our Father knew us. Before we were formed in our mother's womb. He made things ready in advance before He presented us to our parents. He consecrated us and set us apart to His good pleasure. We are not placed or birthed in this world to be the pleasure only for our parents, friends, and mates. The Father's divine purpose and destiny for every person born on the planet would be fulfilled by us receiving Jesus as our Savior. The Bible assures us clearly:

> ... [He] has blessed us with every spiritual blessing in the heavenly realms in Christ, just as [in His love] He chose us in Christ [actually selected us for Himself as His own] before the foundation of the world, so that we would be holy [that is, consecrated, set apart for Him, purpose-driven] and blameless in His sight.

> In love He predestined and lovingly planned for us to be adopted to Himself as [His own] children through Jesus Christ, in accordance with the kind intention and good pleasure of His will— to the praise of His glorious grace and favor, which He so freely bestowed on us in the Beloved [His Son, Jesus Christ].

Joyce B. Respers

In Him we have redemption [that is, our deliverance and salvation] through His blood, [which paid the penalty for our sin and resulted in] the forgiveness and complete pardon of our sin, in accordance with the riches of His grace which He lavished on us.

In all wisdom and understanding [with practical insight] He made known to us the mystery of His will according to His good pleasure, which He purposed in Christ, with regard to the fulfillment of the times [that is, the end of history, the climax of the ages]— to bring all things together in Christ, [both] things in the heavens and things on the earth.

In Him also we have received an inheritance **[a destiny—we were claimed by God as His own],** having been predestined (chosen, appointed beforehand) according to the purpose of Him who works everything in agreement with the counsel and design of His will, so that we who were the first to hope in Christ [who first put our confidence in Him as our Lord and Savior] would exist to the praise of His glory. In Him, you also, when you heard the word of truth, the good news of your salvation, and [as a result] believed in Him, were stamped with the seal of the promised Holy Spirit [the One promised by Christ] as owned and protected [by God].

The Spirit is the guarantee [the first install-ment, the pledge, a foretaste] of our inher-itance until the redemption of God's own [purchased] possession [His believers], to the praise of His glory. *We have been foreor-dained, chosen, and appointed beforehand in accordance with His purpose.* Who works out according to everything in agreement with the counsel and the design of His will. (Ephesians 1:3–14 AMP; emphasis added.)

Some of us may not like the family we are born to; we may not enjoy or embrace the family we are connected with. Or, you might think your arrival was an accident or you are unwanted. The circumstances you are going through is just a smoke screen that satan, the enemy of your soul, is using to confound your mind and move you away from your Creator. The eyes of your understanding are clouded when you do not have any idea who you really are.

Perhaps you see yourself as a misfit. That means you may think you are "a person who does not fit in comfortably with your surroundings, or society; one who cannot conform or adjust to the circumstances in which you live."[34] Believe it or not, this can set anyone up for devastation in their lives.

Trying to fit in the culture today is something we all may be faced with. The major problem is we do not know who we are. It does matter how old you are, what title you possess, how much money you make, or how many degrees you have under your belt. The bottom line is that the world and the Church are both facing this identity crisis.

When we observe the suicide rate, murdering, abuse, alcoholism, and drug usage among most if not all nations today, we must associate this as a severe problem in our society. We must discern the times and the seasons we live in. Satan's job and mandate is to steal, kill, and destroy as many individuals as possible. His strategy is to make it unbearable for all humanity to believe and to receive Jesus.

You may think your only answer is to quit or give up. Don't! You have come across this book for a reason. My voice is hear to tell you that these feelings and thoughts of defeat, despair, and rejection are not preordained thoughts coming from the Father!

Before you go any further, stop thinking about the negative things that satan has put in your mind. The Father wants you to know **you are important**, and **you are not an accident; you are not a mistake**, and **you are not a misfit**.

The truth is... God never created you to fit in with the norm! *You are His masterpiece!* If you are struggling with your identity, you are in a good place for God to lead you to a higher place than yourself. Your mindset must focus on the Kingdom of our dear Lord and not on this world system. God's decree is:

I don't think the way you think. The way you work isn't the way I work.

For as the sky soars high above earth, so the way I work surpasses the way you work, and *the way I think is beyond the way you think.*

Just as rain and snow descend from the skies and don't go back until they've watered the earth, doing their work of making things grow and blossom, producing seed for farmers and food for the hungry,

So will *the words that come out of my mouth not come back empty-handed.*

They'll do the work I sent them to do, they'll complete the assignment I gave them.

(Isaiah 55:8–11 MSG; emphasis added.)

There is a holy assignment and beautiful gifts inside of you that have not been tapped into. It is important that you know who you are in Christ Jesus. God does not want you to spend your entire life trying to figure out who you are. Everything you have gone through has been mere stepping stones to get you to the place where you are right now.

Your season of revelation is upon you. You must understand *your destiny and purpose in life originates in the Father who made you.*

We all have been born in sin and shaped in iniquity through the order of our fallen nature through Adam. "Therefore, just as sin came into the world through [the action of] one man [i. e. , Adam] and [physical] death through that sin, so [physical] death has spread to all people, because all people have sinned" (Romans 5:12 AUV).

But the everlasting good news is that the Father's intention was that Jesus would become the last Adam of the original order. His assignment was purposed in the heart of our Father God to deliver us through the redeeming power of His blood. Jesus, the last Adam, became our substitute in life and death for the payment for sin that the first Adam transferred to the entire globe.

Jesus' destiny and purpose in the Kingdom had to be fulfilled on the cross. This was so that more sons and daughters could be birthed into the Kingdom of God according to God's original desire and design. We may not think we deserve what Jesus has provided for us in His Kingdom. But that is why this is so transforming! It was not of our own works, or merits that we deserve anything, but it is because of what Jesus has done!

Acts 3:19–21 speaks of the time of refreshing and of the times of restoration. Jesus has completed everything to bring restoration and restitution to this lost hurting world. Mankind was lost through sin, neglect, lies, poverty, sickness, and disease. However, through the appointed fullness of time, Jesus showed up on the scene to give us back everything the Father intended for us! And that includes everything that was thwarted in the work of darkness through satan.

This is now the season of restoration, restitution, and refreshing for the church.

The Greek word for *restore* is *apokathístēmi* [Strong's G600] "(from 570 /apistía, "separated from" and 2525 / kathístēmi, "have a definite standing") – properly, restore back to original standing, i.e. that existed before a fall; re-establish, returning back to the (ultimate) ideal; (figuratively) restore back to full freedom (the liberty of the original standing); to enjoy again, i.e. what was taken away by a destructive or life-dominating power.

[Also] 600/apokathistēmi ("reestablish") *emphasizes separation from the former, negative influence* **to enjoy what is forward (the restoration).**"[35]

The Father's desire and purpose have been and always were to have a family in the earth that would be like Him. Jesus, our Lord, made it all possible through His love for His creation, obedience, and submission. His Grace, the unmerited favor of the Father, and compassion met the required need for all mankind.

In restoring mankind back to his original state, it means to put back, to reinstall, to reinstate, to revive, and to recall back to life. We were dead in sin and trespasses. When Adam departed from the original plan God intended, everything fell apart. Sin bought all of creation to an inevitable decline.

But thank God for Jesus! He already knew this was going to happen because He is Omniscient.

Yes, it took forty-two generations for the fullness of time to be manifested. However, His love strengthened Him in restoring us back to our former state. When recognized, believed, and received, the Word has been given and offered to us through the finished work of Jesus. We, the Bride, become pregnant with destiny. The seed of life (Christ Jesus) is planted in our spiritual womb—the hidden treasure within!

The restoration process is to bring us back to our original state from the beginning of creation. Our destiny is already set and positioned in Him (destination). He knew us before the foundation of the worlds were laid (origination). We must give birth to the renewing work of Christ, the hope of glory *Who lives in us.*

You may not have experienced the things I have, but I know that life brings everyone many experiences, challenges and crises. Don't despair and don't give up! Remember His words to you in the Scripture and here in this book, a message to you from Him (through my life):

> I have told you these things, so that in Me you may have [perfect] peace. In the world you have tribulation and distress and suffering, but be courageous [be confident, be undaunted, be filled with joy]; I have overcome the world." [My conquest is accomplished, My victory abiding.] (John 16:33 AMP)

The victory of overcoming is your faith, and it is in knowing your Abba, Daddy God. It is getting to know Him as your expression person, healer, deliverer, savior, and friend through Christ Jesus. You can know Him as your teacher, counselor, comforter, the Spirit of Truth, Grace, your advocate, your helper, intercessor, strengthener and your standby! I am speaking of Holy Spirit, the third person of the Trinity.

John 14:26 says:

> But the Comforter (Counselor, Helper, Intercessor, Advocate, Strengthener, Standby), the Holy Spirit, Whom the Father will send in My name [in My place, to represent Me and act on My behalf], He will teach you all things. And He will cause you to recall (will remind you of, bring to your remembrance) everything I have told you. (AMPC)

So, there we have it. We clearly see in Scripture that we are **destined before birth** and also Scripture is clear that God will cause His purpose to come to pass. Yet, realistically, we know the questions still exist: "Why are we not operating in the fullness of our destiny? And, why are we not bringing forth or birthing our assignments in the Kingdom of God?" The answer to both questions is that we go through life not realizing, not grasping, not laying hold of who we are or what we have been called to do! We can change. He wants to change that revelation in us. It is time to know who we are!

Therefore, if anyone is in Christ, *he is a new creation*; old things have passed away; behold, all things have become new.

Now all things are of God, who has reconciled us to Himself through Jesus Christ, and has given us the ministry of reconciliation, that is, that God was in Christ reconciling the world to Himself, not imputing their trespasses to them, and has committed to us the word of reconciliation.

Now then, we are ambassadors for Christ, as though God were pleading through us: we implore you on Christ's behalf, be reconciled to God.

For He made Him who knew no sin to be sin for us, *that we might become the righteousness of God in Him.* (2 Corinthians 5:17–21 NKJV; emphasis added)

Chapter 13

The New Vessel

What revelation have you discovered about yourself in the Kingdom thus far? Are you still questioning your purpose? Have you been left motionless trying to fit in and be accepted by your peers, friends, Pastor, spouse, or people on your job? Have you been condemning yourself about your issues? What about comparing your life with everyone around you?

Or perhaps you struggle from another angle. You may have asked these questions: Is it fine for me to desire to see myself confident, courageous, and fearless? Is it wrong to think that I am righteous or to see myself bold and walking in the authority that has been allotted to me? How can I be anointed? How can I be God's Ambassador (His representative) when I do not possess the ability or know how to function in my call and setting?

If your answer to any of these questions is yes, this chapter will be what you need to set you free from the bondages you have been carrying all the days of your existence. Are you going to keep denying who the Father called and created you to be in his kingdom? Will you continue to think you are incapable or not good enough to be released in His ministry? Holy Spirit wants you to know that if you are born again, you are a son of God in His Kingdom, and you are righteous. *The Righteousness of God is who you are.* He is consistently equipping you for the tasks at hand for the work of the ministry.

You possess the nature of the Righteousness of God; therefore, He has deposited everything in you to fulfill His purpose and destiny in your life. However, the spirit of guilt, rejection, and condemnation will always leave us as cowards and as prisoners of satan. The confidence that Jesus has given you is for you to believe and rest in your Righteousness. The process of learning and understanding your personal relationship with Him will cause you to know who you are positionally in your Righteousness.

He is equipping you in His ministry of excellence. In the process of maturing, we must agree with the Father about who He said we are in His Kingdom. You may say, "Is it pride if I think what He says about me? Is it ok? Will I be arrogant if I agree with Him?" If you are struggling with your identity, as I struggled with mine, you can rest assured Jesus is here to help you through your dilemma. Let's look at how Jesus dealt with thoughts:

> Who, being in the form of God, thought it not robbery to be equal with God: but made himself of no reputation, and took upon him

the form of a servant, and was made in the likeness of men: and being found in fashion as a man, he humbled himself, and became obedient unto death, even the death of the cross. (Philippians 2:6–8)

Jesus was God encased in flesh yet without sin. However, He did not think of Himself as robbing the Glory from God by thinking equality with God. What did He do? He walked in humility. He became a servant. He was obedient to everything the Father told Him to do or say, even unto the point of death. We are to follow this same pattern from His example in our identity. Jesus is our great high priest officiating in us, His Temple, and reconciling us to our original form. This is our original state from the beginning before Adam and Eve failed in the garden.

What actually is *righteousness?* Righteousness, according to Merriam Webster, is acting in accord with divine or moral law, free from guilt or sin, and morally right or justifiable.[36]

The Word of the Lord has a lot to say about being made righteous. The Scripture is packed with rich inspiration and revelation that will result in salvation for everyone who chooses to believe and receive this truth.

For with the heart a person believes in Christ as Savior resulting in his justification that is, being made righteous—being freed of the guilt of sin and made acceptable to God; and

with the mouth he acknowledges and con-
fesses his faith openly, resulting in and con-
firming [his] salvation. (Romans 10:10 AMP)

The first prerequisite is to choose to believe in the finished work Jesus has completed on our behalf. His love for
The Father and for us was His motivation that caused Him
to go to Calvary for us. In the book *Perelandra*, C. S. Lewis
wrote:

> When He died in the Wounded World, He
> died not for men, but for each man. If each
> man had been the only man made, He would
> have done no less.

What a profound statement of Truth! "He died not for
men, but for **each man**. If each man had been the only man
made, He would have done no less." He died to redeem me
if no other person ever chose to receive Him as Savior and
Lord. **He died to redeem you** if no other person ever chose
to receive Him as Savior and Lord.

The challenge comes in accepting that we could not do
and cannot do anything to *earn* this redemption and righteousness. The Mosaic Law, through the blood sacrifice of
many animals, was unable to bring us salvation, freedom, deliverance, and healing. The Law was only a pointer, a revealer
or an indicator to show us what sin looked like. But Jesus is
the fulfillment and the culmination of the Law. In what the

Law could not do, Jesus became our propitiation. Our only part is to **receive His gift. Don't struggle. It is a gift.**

Here is where many my run into a religious problem. We have been told by religion we must keep going back to the altar and do our first work of repentance every time we mess up, even though we are saved! Most people were never taught that once we are redeemed, the new life and nature of God **made us righteous.** Philippians 1:11 (AMP) says we are to be...

> ...filled with the fruit of righteousness which comes through Jesus Christ, to the glory and praise of God so that His glory may be both revealed and recognized.

For centuries, man-made religion has blinded the minds of God's people. The spirit of law and condemnation has kept us carnal, fruitless, fearful, and faithless for too long. *Think about it.* If all you think about is your issues, your sins, your faults, and mishaps, there is a problem, my beloved. This is called **sin consciousness.** E. W. Kenyon addressed both topics, sin consciousness and righteousness in his writings and sermons delivered during the first half of the twentieth century. Here are two quotes of impact:

> The dominion of a sin consciousness over the Church has been fostered, developed, and made a reality by ministers who have

preached sin instead of preaching Christ and the new creation. When we received Jesus as our Lord and Savior, we received the nature of God, and we are automatically the righteousness of God in Christ Jesus. Spiritually dead men cannot stand in God's presence.[37]

Until a man knows that he is the righteousness of God, he will never take advantage of his privileges. He will always live in bondage to the enemy.[38]

Once we acknowledge God as our loving Father and accept Jesus as our Lord and Savior, His Word (as we allow it) will dispel every lie and negative word satan brings to our minds. The truth is that Jesus has justified us through the power of His love. His Word brings light and truth to our minds and lives.

In essence, righteousness means the ability to stand in the presence of God our Father without guilt, condemnation, or inferiority. We must believe it, confess it, and stand on this truth. According to the scriptures, we do not have to wait until we die to become righteous! We do not have to go to heaven to become saints. We are already what our Father said we are... *sons.* This is a new creation reality present in us now.

There is therefore now no condemnation to those who are in Christ Jesus, who do not

> walk according to the flesh, but according to
> the Spirit. For the law of the Spirit of life in
> Christ Jesus has made me free from the law of
> sin and death. (Romans 8:1–2 NKJV)

> Therefore, brethren, we are debtors—not to
> the flesh, to live according to the flesh. For if
> you live according to the flesh you will die;
> but if by the Spirit you put to death the deeds
> of the body, you will live. For as many as are
> led by the Spirit of God, these are sons of God.
> (Romans 8:12–14 NKJV)

The life and the nature of the old man under sin and death has been dealt with through the blood of Jesus. Jesus, through redemption, has completely destroyed our sin nature. We now have the nature of Christ Jesus living in us.

We are to recognize our sonship, the relationship as provided by Christ Jesus in us. Once we realize what we have in Christ, He enables us to share the effectual working of our believing the Word of God. God committed His righteousness to us. The fruit of righteousness is located in us and it is the manifestation on the glorified Christ in us that is being revealed.

We grow in our sonship. As believers, in Jesus we have received everything that pertain to life and godliness. We are like our Father from on high. He is full of ability and power, and because He offers that potential to us, as we choose Him, so are we. As His sons, we have access to everything that our Father has given us. We are laborers and joint heirs with Jesus.

> ... so that He might sanctify the church, having cleansed her by the washing of water with the word of God, so that in turn He might present the church to Himself in glorious splendor, without spot or wrinkle or any such thing; but that she would be holy, set apart for God, and blameless. (Ephesians 5:26–27 AMP)

We have become the righteous in Christ Jesus; the Divine Nature of Jesus has been infused in us. As believers, we possess the nature of our Father. The Holy God of all creation resides in us as His dwelling place.

This new man, the newly created vessel, complete with the new nature in God is being transformed from the inside out! Old things are passed away and I am who He said I am. I can do what He said I can do—and so can you if you believe and receive Him, accepting sonship by recognizing who you are in Christ our Lord!

Now faith is. Now. We must stand in stability and truth of our identity formed *in the Maker's hands*—immediately upon acknowledging the free gift of salvation, receiving Christ as Lord and Savior, ***we are the righteousness of Jesus Christ.***

Chapter 14
Staying in the Maker's Hands

Life is about the journey that we all must take. We begin with learning who we are and understanding how we got here. We continue, ever learning by experiencing and getting acquainted with our true worth and value, as we journey toward the revelation and understanding of our purpose. This is the intent of our Heavenly Father for our lives.

Each individual must resolve within yourselves there is someone greater than you. We have a heavenly Father who was moved with compassion **to choose us** to love. Sadly, many people allow excuses for our hidden issues and demons within to prevent us from believing and receiving His Love and from being able to flow in our divine destiny! If not addressed in agreement with God's Word, even the relationships we have with our earthly family and others may have a diabolical influence (evil, devilish) on our behavior and attitude.

The truth is that no one's bad attitude and negative behavior should ever be used as an excuse to keep one out of the Kingdom of our dear Lord. In spite of all of our idiosyncrasies, faults, and weaknesses, *He saw something beautiful in the clay He chose.* Hidden within each one of us is a glorious treasure that is waiting to be exposed and revealed to the world.

In His innermost depths, Jesus yearned to fulfill His divine purpose in His creation. It is often written of Jesus that He was moved with compassion or that He had great compassion.

> Wherefore in all things it behooved Him to be made like unto His brethren, that He might be a merciful *[compassionate]* and faithful High Priest. (Hebrews 2:17; emphasis added.)

Why did Jesus endure such an awesome ordeal as Calvary? There was one basic reason. *He was moved with compassion!* And He is still moved with compassion... **for you.**

Devastations come to bring ruin by violent actions to our lives. They may come in the form of molestation, abuse, murder, rejection, sickness, storms, and famine. The list is endless; nevertheless, the main purpose of devastation from the enemy is to create chaos, catastrophe, and disorder in our environment and lives.

You may have had a very hard life. You may be experiencing sufferings or going through some type of discomfort right now. Know this beloved: Jesus will be with you in the midst of it all! Settle that in your heart. He loves you. Call to Him for comfort and help. He is faithful and compassionate.

It is of utmost importance that we learn and believe that God does not put devastation upon us nor does He cause illness or destruction in our lives. It is the enemy who comes to steal, kill, and destroy. God will walk you through those times into your victory.

Knowing that, and knowing our Master Potter has good for us all our days, we can also acknowledge that there can be trials, discomforts, or challenges that indicate the Father has you in the furnace or fire to burn up the chaff (unnecessary, unfruitful parts) and remove the dross (impurities) in your life. Or it could be that He is using the two-edge sword (His Word) to chisel out the clay and remove the useless residue or impurities from your past that has been keeping you from maturity.

Paul, an apostle (and the writer of the majority of what we now know as the New Testament), suffered greatly in many tribulations, yet he still declared:

> I count all things but loss for the excellency of the knowledge of Christ Jesus my Lord: for whom I have suffered the loss of all things, and do count them but dung, that I may win Christ... [and] that I may know him, and the power of his resurrection, and the fellowship of his sufferings, being made conformable unto his death. (Philippians 3:8, 10)

In other words, Paul was saying, "I want to be a partaker of His suffering. I want to be so acquainted and in harmony with Him until I am fully formed into His image." Paul's trials and suffering were horrific. Yet his love relationship with God provoked him to want to be fashioned like Christ for a similar purpose as our Lord. He wrote in Philippians 1:21-26 (NIV; emphasis added) about *staying in the Maker's hands*, living the life worthy of the Gospel:

> For to me, to live is Christ and to die is gain. If I am to go on living in the body, this will mean fruitful labor for me. Yet what shall I choose? I do not know! I am torn between the two: I desire to depart and be with Christ, which is better by far; but it is more necessary for you that I remain in the body. Convinced of this, I know that I will remain, and *I will continue with all of you for your progress and joy in the faith, so that through my being with you again your boasting in Christ Jesus will abound on account of me.*

As Great High Priest, Jesus suffered the death for sin so that we do not have to suffer it. Trials, devastation, pain and heartache will be a part of our life's journey. Yet, Jesus' promises are sure. In Hebrews 13:5 (NKJV; emphasis added),

"He Himself has said, 'I will never leave you nor forsake you.'"

This world is incessantly changing. People are constantly leaving, whether it's death or other broken relationships. Yet God's promise to never leave us is encouraging. We are endlessly being processed by the Master Potter during this journey. Just as the Father was in Jesus during His journey, when we receive Jesus as Lord and Savior, the fullness of the Godhead dwells in us as well.

> God was in Christ, reconciling the world unto Himself. (2 Corinthians 5:19)

What lesson is there for us in this? **Through it all, we must seize the revelation from our Father that life is not over in the midst of the devastation, *but deliverance is at hand!* We are now partakers of this divine experience. We have the fullness of the Godhead dwelling in us.**

> In Him we live, and move, and have our being. (Acts 17:28)

> I am crucified with Christ: nevertheless I live; yet not I, but Christ liveth in me: and the life which I now live in the flesh I live by the faith of the Son of God, who loved me, and gave himself for me. (Galatians 2:20)

It is not I that lives, but it is Christ Jesus who now lives in me.

Paul remained focused in His divine assignment. Like Jesus, he refused to bail out—he was set on staying *in the Maker's hands.* Yes, like Paul, we are often facing devastations, trails, crisis, and tests, but we must realize the benefits will outweigh all the negative we are facing. We must endure with travail, as a woman travails to birth her child. When it is over, what a beautiful result. You may see the test, the trials and circumstances as an awful experience, but instead Jesus wants us to remain steadfast and faithful through it all. We have been united with Him and we get to share in His suffering. Yes, how outstanding this is! A chance to share in His glory as well!

When it appears that we are approaching the finish line of a particular season in our destiny or assignment, all hell seems to burst forth. Can I say, "Welcome to your Calvary experience!" The purpose of the Calvary experience was first conceived in our Lord Jesus. What did He do during this experience? He chose to dig deep into the Glory of the Father by showing mercy and forgiveness. He was moved with compassion to save humanity. He remained right there *in the Maker's hands,* even to death on that Cross until all was completed.

Likewise, do not allow what you are facing to keep you from realizing who you really are to God. The new life of Christ in you is waiting to be manifested. It is during these moments of difficulties the Father is calling you in to His throne room, the most intimate place of consecration where He will reveal His secrets to you. Jesus wants you to remain focused and *stay in the Master's hand* until your season of fulfillment arrives. You may be wondering when will your best life ever arrive. You might be asking, "How long, Lord?" Or, "When God? When?" Rest assured that it is fine to ask your Father these questions as long as you willingly listen for His answer! Romans 8:26–28 (NIV) says,

> In the same way, the Spirit helps us in our weakness. We do not know what we ought to pray for, but the Spirit himself intercedes for us through wordless groans. And he who searches our hearts knows the mind of the Spirit, because the Spirit intercedes for God's people in accordance with the will of God. And we know that in all things God works for the good of those who love him, who have been called according to his purpose.

First things first! If you are not a believer, and you have read through this entire book to this point, beloved, this is the time for you to look to Jesus as your source for your destiny and His assignment for your life. Let Him be your Savior and Lord of your Life. Right now. This very moment.

Jesus is calling to your heart. He is waiting for you to align your faith to totally trust Him. He is moved with compassion to rescue you. He hears your cry and He has seen your tears and restless life. He is moved with compassion to meet all of your needs despite what weaknesses you may be facing.

Life, as I mentioned earlier, is a journey. We are on this journey, and you will never have to be alone—right now, you can allow Him free access! Let Him come—invite Him—into your life and take residence within. Put your life *in the Maker's hands* and allow Him to chisel, prepare, shape, smooth, and even fire you into the finished work, His beautiful vessel of honor.

If you know Him as Lord and Savior already, this is an opportunity for true breakthrough! Be soluble once again! But know this: getting or obtaining your breakthrough is not a cliche to be thrown around. It is not something to say to make others think you have arrived. Do not use satires to impress anyone. The irony in the church today is that many are saying they are free, delivered, and walking in their purpose and the promises of God, but the truth is that the body of Christ is still devastated from poor self-image because she doesn't know who she is. The members of the Body of Christ are vacillating from one realm to another trying to find their identity.

This is your defining moment! Begin to learn who you are as a believer. Learn to submit to your spiritual leaders and become a student of the kingdom. Study the Word of God and begin renewing your mind daily. True deliverance from life's devastation occurs when we are honest and confess, "Lord, I don't know who I really am!" When we get tired of perpetrating a fraud, being fake, being impostors, and following the pattern of other unconditioned clay! Humbly return to that soluble greenware, raw clay *in the Maker's hands.*

This is where we can say, "Abba, Daddy, I need you to make me over—a new vessel, a new creation *in the Maker's hands.*"

Second, it is imperative for you to get your mind off of you. We are all being molded. Jesus is able to take care of the residue that may be hanging around in the soulish man. Our part is to recognize that Jesus' ministry is located in us! We must develop the pattern of being concerned about someone other than ourselves. We are His sons aligning with our identity in our Father's Kingdom. Yes, we are maturing in that because maturity enables us to agree with the divine calling and assignment.

Once you decide to receive Jesus as Lord and Savior the seed of Life is in you. Total restoration may now begin. It is walking in the process of being perfected or matured. Know that you will face the circumstances of life. You may see them in a way that may cause you great pain. They can often be events or situations that you cannot control. However, our attitude and choices are to continue to believe God, and to serve faithfully in the midst of these circumstances.

Circumstances occur in life are part of the journey. When they appear, they are markers or indicators to show us our level of maturity in the Kingdom. How we handle them will determine our level of leadership, love, commitment, and faithfulness to Jesus, to others, and to His ministry. Remember, the battle is not yours! It has never been yours to fight—the battle belongs to our Father.

My parting words to you are to assure you that God has purposed and chosen you. He chiseled you out even as raw,

147

unconditioned clay. He prepared you for your journey. He has given His children the authority in His kingdom—authority to do great exploits in the assignment!

Your life is not over yet. Truly today it can be a new beginning *in the Maker's hands*. Take what you have read (heard) in these pages and move forward. Ask God to turn your tragedy into triumph, and watch Him cause you to laugh and dance your way into victory.

No matter what age you are or how long you have been in the Lord, He promises us that His glorious vessel is still being shaped and smoothed for honorable use! Stay ***In the Maker's Hands*** and let Jesus show you ***how to turn devastation to breakthrough and shape your best life!***

Notes

1   PsychologyDiscussion.net   "Reasoning: Meaning, Definition and Types," August 17, 2016. http://www.psychologydiscussion.net/thinking/reasoning-meaning-definition-and-types/2060.

2   "Definition of Acquainted." Accessed August 22, 2022.   https://www.merriam-webster. com/dictionary/acquainted.

3   https://www.   cbcmidway.   org/2011/01/08/bible-study-the-five-stages-of-spiritual-growth

4   Strong's Greek: 3516. Νήπιος (Népios) -- an Infant, Fig. a Simple-Minded or Immature Person." Accessed August 22, 2022. https://biblehub. com/greek/3516.htm 2

5   Fit: FIT | English meaning - Cambridge Dictionary. https://dictionary.cambridge.org/dictionary/english/fit

6   Career Explorer, "What Does a Potter Do?" Career Explorer, April 11, 2017, https://www. careerexplorer.com/careers/potter/.

7   Morris, Hubert A. Jesus and His Covenant. 1980. Reprint, Vanceboro, N. C. : Highlights Publisher, 1985.

8   Strong's Hebrew: 6083. (APHAR) -- Dry Earth, dust, accessed July 2, 2023, https://biblehub.com/hebrew/6083.htm.

9   Ask Difference. "Clay vs. Mud - What's the Difference?" Accessed September 1, 2022. http://www. askdifference.com/clay-vs-mud/

10   Julia Blum, "Beginnings (9) : Genesis 2," Biblical Hebrew and Holy Land Studies Blog - IIBS.com (The Israel Institute of Biblical Studies, February 27, 2020), https://blog.israelbiblicalstudies.com/jewish-studies/beginnings-9-genesis-2/.

11 Merriam-Webster.com Dictionary, s.v. "impostor," accessed May 7, 2023, https://www.merriam-webster.com/dictionary/impostor.

12 Merriam-Webster.com Dictionary, s.v. "pretender," accessed May 7, 2023, https://www.merriam-webster.com/dictionary/pretender.

13 Merriam-Webster.com Dictionary, s.v. "imitator," accessed May 7, 2023, https://www.merriam-webster.com/dictionary/imitator

14 Merriam-Webster.com Dictionary, s.v. "trickster," accessed May 7, 2023, https://www.merriam-webster.com/dictionary/trickster

15 "Pottery as Art: Collections." In The Italic People of Ancient Apulia, 281–302. Cambridge University Press, 2014. http://dx. doi. org/10. 1017/cbo9781107323513. 026.

16 Strong, James. The New Strong's Expanded Exhaustive Concordance of the Bible. Red lettered. Nashville, Tenn.: Thomas Nelson, 2010. s. v."nēpios" (n).

17 Strong's Greek: 3813. Παιδίον (Paidion) -- a Young Child." Accessed August 22, 2022. https://biblehub. com/ greek/3813. htm.

18 "Definition of Clay." Accessed August 31, 2022. https://www. Merriam-webster. com/dictionary/clay.

19 Strong's Greek: 3516. Νήπιος (Népios) -- an Infant, Fig. a Simple-Minded or Immature Person." Accessed August 22, 2022. https://biblehub. com/greek/3516.htm 2

20 Ron Graham, "Filthy Rags-Isaiah 64:4-9," Filthy Rags - Isaiah 64:4-9, 2001, https://www.simplybible.com/f924-isaiah64-filthy-rags.htm.

21 Merriam-Webster.com Dictionary, s.v."produce," accessed May 7, 2023, https://www.merriam-webster.com/dictionary/produce.

22 Merriam-Webster.com Dictionary, s.v."sanctify," accessed May 7, 2023, https://www.merriam-webster.com/dictionary/sanctify.

23 Science Is Simple."Atoms," August 20, 2019. https:// scienceissimple. com/atoms/.

24 Mackinnon, Lesley. "3 Stages of Firing Clay – a Beginners Guide to Firing Pottery," Pottery Tips by The Pottery Wheel, July 15, 2022, https://thepotterywheel.com/stages-of-firing-clay/.

25 Ibid.

26 Ibid.

27 Ibid.

28 Mackinnon, Lesley A. "What Is the First Firing of Clay Called? - Bisque, Biscuit or Bisc?" Pottery Tips by The

Pottery Wheel, July 15, 2022. https://thepotterywheel.com/what-is-the-first-firing-of-clay-called/.

29 Mackinnon. "3 Stages of Firing Clay – a Beginners Guide to Firing Pottery."

30 Smithsonian Magazine, "Diamonds Unearthed," Smithsonian.com, December 1, 2006, https://www.smithsonianmag.com/science-nature/diamonds-un-earthed-141629226/.

31 The Discovery Bible, "HELPS Word Studies," Strong's Greek: 3339. μεταμορφόω (metamorphoó) -- to transform, 2021, https://biblehub.com/greek/3339.htm.

32 Merriam-Webster.com Dictionary, s.v. "metamorphose," accessed August 1, 2023, https://www.merriam-webster.com/dictionary/metamorphose.

33 Merriam-Webster.com Dictionary, s.v. "destiny," accessed August 1, 2023, https://www.merriam-webster.com/dictionary/destiny.

34 Sergey Poznyakoff, "GNU Collaborative International Dictionary of English," misfit - GNU Collaborative International Dictionary of English, accessed August 1, 2023, https://gcide.gnu.org.ua/?q=misfit&define=Define&strategy=.

35 BibleHub, "HELPS Word-Studies," Strong's greek: 600. ἀποκαθίστημι (apokathistémi) -- to restore, give back, 2021, https://biblehub.com/greek/600.htm.

36 Merriam-Webster.com Dictionary, s.v. "righteous," accessed May 7, 2023, https://www.merriam-webster.com/dictionary/righteous.

37 Kenyon, E. W. Two Kind of Righteousness. Reprint, Lynwood, Washington: Kenyon's Gospel Publishing Society, Inc., 1996.

38 Kenyon, E. W. A New Kind of Christianity.

Special Tribute

The unique cover art of this book was inspired by the original concept of the author's granddaughter, Kamiyah Terrilee Russsell Respers. This young woman of God is a gifted aspiring artist that the Lord is using in these last days. Her original concept piece is pictured here (in greyscale) as a tribute (with parental permission) and with the author's loving thanks.

Meet the Author

Born Joyce Marie Blount and raised in Maribel, North Carolina, the author is the daughter of Clarence W. Blount (deceased) and Mattie Jones Blount. She is the wife of Billy E. Respers. A native of Pamlico County for 35 years, Dr. Respers and her husband presently reside in New Bern, North Carolina. From their union, they have three adult children, Kristen Joy, Christopher Cornelius, and Dejulo Lamont Respers (deceased) and nine grandchildren.

She earned her Theology degree (1982) from the Nondenominational Bible Institute (NDBI) of James City, North Carolina. She earned a Master of Education (2012) with a concentration in Family Community Services from Ashford University. She received her Master of Theology (2015) and her Ph.D. (2023) from Bible Faith Global University.

Dr. Joyce Respers has been an educator for more than four decades, teaching Language Arts and Social Studies with Craven County and Pamlico County School Systems. She is presently the U.S. Chancellor of Bible Faith Global University. In that capacity, she serves as administrator and online professor for all who desire to further their studies in the Kingdom of God.

Joyce (Blount) Respers received salvation under the ministry of Senior Pastor Dr. Willie Grant in 1977 and was called into the ministry in 1981. Entering ministry in 1982, she taught English for three years while working at NDBI, assisting students in receiving their GED.

Dr. Respers and her husband Elder Billy Respers are the Founders and former Pastors of Family Outreach Word of Deliverance Ministries Incorporated, established in 1991. The Ministry's foundation scripture is Isaiah 58:12 (emphasis added),

> *And they that shall be of thee shall build the old waste places; they shall raise up the foundation of many generations; and be called The Repairer the breech, The restorer of paths to dwell in.*

Apostle Dr. Joyce Respers is resolute in her faith and about helping the Body of Christ to learn how to study and understand the Word of God. Continuing in that desire to connect with others sharing the same Spirit, Apostle Respers became a member of I AM Ministries in 2014 under the leadership of Apostle Dr. Alfred Kornegay.

Dr. Respers believes that time is of the essence for God's people to grow, mature, and complete their assignment in the Body of Christ. She is a woman of God that loves the Lord, loves to hear from God, and desires to please Jesus with all her heart. Her prayer for all who come across this book is her favorite scripture in Isaiah 40:31 (emphasis added),

> *But those who hope in the Lord will renew their strength. They will soar on wings like eagles; they will run and not grow weary; they will walk and not be faint.*

To invite Apostle Dr. Joyce Respers to speak or
to purchase additional copies,
please visit :

familyoutreachministry.com

You may contact the author directly:

Dr. Joyce B. Respers
Family Outreach WORD Ministries
PO Box 3442
New Bern NC 28364

www.ingramcontent.com/pod-product-compliance
Lightning Source LLC
Chambersburg PA
CBHW051520120626
46551CB00012B/1014